WAKE UP AND WRITE

HOW TO WRITE PROLIFICALLY

An "inspirational" and practical book
for all writers and would-be writers

by William Manners

ARCO PUBLISHING COMPANY, Inc.
219 Park Avenue South, New York, N.Y. 10003

This one is for Jane

Third Edition, Second Printing, 1978

Published by Arco Publishing Company, Inc.
219 Park Avenue South, New York, N.Y. 10003

Library of Congress Cataloging in Publication Data

Manners, William, 1907-
  Wake up and write.

  Includes bibliographical references.
  1. Authorship.   I. Title.

PN147.M36   1976   808'.042   76-26150
ISBN 0-668-04093-9 (Paperback Edition)

Printed in the United States of America

Preface

WHEN I was a child, and reading fairy tales, I had a frightening problem. What, I asked myself, if someone, for some reason—as in a fairy tale—were suddenly to appear and give me three wishes? I had read enough to know that an individual had only one such offer in a lifetime. Understandably, I got busy trying to figure out the best possible three wishes. There were obvious ones, like having all the candy I wanted, but apprehensive that I might be making the wrong choice, I continued to worry and think.

Finally, I was ready for the beneficent one. Let him come. My first wish would be for everything. My second wish would be to have the right to reserve the third wish for the time that something might possibly go wrong with my number one wish.

Where wishing is concerned, I had realized, being all-inclusive is all-important. This truism applies generally and to all men. When a freelance writer's wife, for example, asked her husband what he wanted for his birthday, he said—and he was poignantly serious, too—"I want to be prolific like Trollope, Simenon and that crowd."

3

(It would obviously have been a sad mistake if he had merely asked that a particular script of his be bought for a good price.)

It is common knowledge that everyone is—or thinks he is—a writer; so this book is for everyone, and may conceivably make many writers' wishes come true, including the "to-be-prolific" one. Appropriately, it will have a magical formula for that particular wish, one that I uncovered by years of probing as a writer and as the former editor of *Alfred Hitchcock's Mystery Magazine*.

And though everyone writes, they also, paradoxically, and for varying intervals, do not write. There are those who want to write, but can't; those who should be able to write, but won't (they're afraid to); those who can write, but don't.

The "not-writing" pain is so excruciating that I feel justified in adopting certain shady means toward alleviating it. The tone of the book, for one thing, may be somewhat inspirational; it may also at times partake of the bullying of a coach between halves, who in order to restore the will to win in his dispirited players resorts to profanity and ad hominem that vehemently ricochets off the lockers.

But inspiration has the drawback of being short-lived and in need of constant renewal, which takes time—time better spent at the typewriter. And in order to keep you productively at the typewriter —the intent of this book—there is also a hard factual core. And it will concern itself with fiction rather than nonfiction, for fiction is more difficult; and what applies to it will, in great measure, apply to nonfiction.

In presenting these facts, I have taken certain liberties. I employ generalities, but merely as an expedient. Oversimplification also springs from necessity. And since I know that if you are to set yourself up as an authority, the first thing that you should do is sound like one, I have done that.

I would also like to say a few words about the book's title. Though there's truth in it, it may have the unpleasant ring of hard and soft sells. It is not unusual, you must remember, for publishers to consult with their sales force about a book's title. They want the title to help sell the book, by being catchy or provocative; they also want it to make clear precisely what is being sold. And so we have WAKE UP AND WRITE.

Contents

Chapter One

HOW TO APPROACH
WRITING POSITIVELY

WHY should one writer's writing crawl, while another's gallops? It's really something of a psychological mystery. X will do a novelette over a week end. Y, on the other hand, has been dawdling on a play for years. "Just been working on it in odd moments," he says. "When the spirit moves me; it's just a hobby." Another Y produces, but slowly, painfully slowly. Z writes nothing at all, hates his wife and children—even himself. Another Z is not working because he wrote a book and it was published and he is spending all his time reading what the critics had to say about it and pasting their comments in a scrap book.

He's so in love with this published work of his, that to start on something else would be tantamount to adultery or bigamy.

The one thing that prolific X has that the other writers do not have is confidence. He may also have drive and alimony payments to meet. The Y's and Z's may also have these, but the one thing they do not have is X's confidence.

X may be confident because of his success (or productivity), but he is also successful or productive because of his confidence. Evidently, not all circles are vicious.

To be prolific—let us grasp hands tightly and make the deductive leap together—one must have a positive or confident approach to one's writing, rather than a negative or defeatist approach.

"But everything I write is junk. So what have I got to be confident about?" (This is but one cry to arise. And it's a negative one—a very good example of a negative one.)

"How am I going to be confident?" (This one's not quite as negative, if the tone expresses a genuine interest. Of course, if bellowed belligerently, it's an entirely different matter.)

"Maybe I ought to forget about writing. Be something wholesome like an elder statesman. Or get a job in a factory—where you can forget about confidence and all such tenuous nonsense." Free - lance writers everywhere will recognize this jeremiad; it is made by free-lance writers everywhere, when the writing isn't going well or a rejection has just been received. Wives of free-lance writers everywhere will know what it means should the husband add to the above, "You know it might be very interesting to work in a joint where they split the atom, or be an orderly in a mental hospital. There are a lot of ways beside writing to make a living. There sure are. Who needs it?" This means he's already wondering if he couldn't get a book out of a stint in an atom-splitting establishment or in a mental hospital. She has also found that her best—though far from satisfactory—reply is a humoring, "Yes, dear."

There are very definite positive attitudes towards one's work which one may cultivate. And here are ten of them:

1. It is not difficult to assume the bearing of confidence. Your posture and expression shouldn't make it appear that you're transporting an outsized cross. The confident person is a relaxed person; to the extent to which you're relaxed, you'll be confident. But the one who lacks confidence is tense with wondering if he can do what he's trying to do; if it will be well received if and when he does it; if, should he do it, he will be able to follow it up with something else that proves that he deserved to be heralded as a writer of promise.

2. Some writers write best when the novel they're doing is under contract, or—if it's an article, it has been assigned to them. In lieu of a contract or an assignment, try this: Tell yourself that you'd better get on with whatever you happen

to be doing, for such and such a publisher is waiting for your script. You then have more reason to proceed full speed ahead. Dallying—except for those who have a taste for it—is an expression of doubt and uncertainty. Of course your admonition should not be hollow; it should have the solidity of belief. There is a decided difference between deluding yourself and believing in yourself.

3. To put yourself in the prolific, confident frame of mind, it's wise to have a few projects going. And if you happen to be working on something big, at least have something else ready to get started on when you're finished. (One successful, and prolific, novelist said that he couldn't finish all that he has lined up for himself even if he lived longer than he should.)

4. If you get stuck while plotting a particular short story, really stuck, instead of letting this throw you into a well of gloom, drop the troublesome, dead-end plot and start immediately on an entirely different story. Your attitude should be devil-may-care rather than worried. So what if a certain tack doesn't work out? The number of plot ideas is infinite, as are the ways in which they may be resolved.

5. Reading is all right as long as it does not become a substitute for writing. The good that you read will inspire; the bad, encourage.

6. Approach a job with disdain rather than temerity. The former is the attitude of the master; the latter that of the incompetent. The feeling

that you can do better than what has been done in the particular area in which you're working —even if you definitely can't—is the right frame of mind.

7. Proceed, steadily, at your individual pace. Tales about prolific writers—made taller frequently by publicity people—can have a very deleterious effect on a writer not satisfied with his output. They can make him hurry—and straight to confusion. More important than brute speed is that you keep working. This doesn't mean that the slow writer should wallow in his slowness and feel that it is that which distinguishes him from the rest of writing mankind. Usually the slow writer is the sensitive writer—the particularly sensitive writer. To him the leaf floating past his study window makes the power-thrust zoom of a jet and when its landing shakes the earth, he falls to the floor, face down and at full length, and lies prone until the tremors stop. Of course, after such an experience he cannot do any work for some time. Even before the leaf fell and before he could get started working, everything must be optimum for such a writer—each mouse must be in its respective hole and the barometric pressure must be just so.

8. Do one part of a job at a time, with sure, straight-forward dispatch. Don't be forever fretting about the whole, about what is yet to be done.

9. You should reach a point, a psychic point, at which you honestly believe you can solve any writing problem that arises. The answer to a

particular problem may not come at once, but past experience has shown you that it will come; the important thing is that you be patient and keep your confidence intact.

10. You must assume that your taste is good. You must also assume that what you like others will also like. (Fortunately, the taste of others doesn't have to be as good as yours, for this to be true.)

But just as one may approach one's work in these ten positive ways, there are innumerable ways in which a writer may be negative rather than positive. And the good writer, the imaginative, creative writer or the potentially good writer, is unfortunately adept at finding these negative devices and using them. Here are a few by way of illustration.

1. We constantly receive manuscripts with accompanying timid letters. "Dear Editor," they say, "this is the first story I have ever written and probably shouldn't have, but I have so would you please waste a little of your precious time in reading it? After you've read it, I know you'll want to return it in the stamped, self addressed envelope. Would you please, sir, tell me why it's no good? I'd just like to know what makes it so terrible."

A very kind and understanding rejection slip must of necessity go to this writer who glories in his negativeness. And because it happens to be printed rather than typed, does not detract from the editor's solicitude. Much thought went into the composition of that printed rejection slip, for it was not done for one writer, but for a timeless, untold number.

2. It is not good to be forever putting off writing. This is usually the delay of fear. If you don't start, fear admonishes, you won't fail; if you do start, you may fail. And so you're safe as long as you can put off writing.

Just as there are some artists who never stop going to art school, so there are writers who are always tracking down an illusive treatment or finding precisely the right names for their characters or doing research. Interminable research is an especially good device, for it is long wearing and makes you feel like a scholar instead of the bum you really know you are.

One historical novelist has this positive, commercial approach. "People," he maintains, "were no different in the past than they are now." (What normal street doesn't have its Becky Sharp or Scarlett O'Hara?) So this writer believes you should write as though you're writing about your contemporaries. Afterwards, you can always, after a day or so at the appropriate museum, go back and, with pastry tube in hand, lay on the historical trimming.

Another novelist—this one nonhistorical—gets what research material he needs by brain picking someone who has specialized information he needs. Though he usually takes his victim to lunch, this doesn't stop him from firing away with his questions, nor does the transparency of his motives cause him shame. This lunch-interview over, the writer regards himself as an authority. He goes so far as to tell the person he's interviewed some things he's just learned as though they were his own. This may not be pure dedicated research —some may even view it with a distaste—but there is a moral here for the non-writing writer, hamstrung by research.

3. Sometimes writers will attempt to do a short story before they have a story to tell. All they have is an extremely intriguing beginning, a narrative hook sort of thing, the nude woman (Isn't a nude always a woman?) who is creeping about on the uppermost ledge of a 45-story building. They don't know who the woman is, why she is nude, why she is in such an unusual place for a nude. A writer should not resort to this sort of thing. He should have enough confidence in himself to patiently figure out a story, from its beginning to its conclusion. When he doesn't have such confidence, he probably hasn't been writing and feels that he should be writing and so this is the sort of thing to which he resorts. Moreover, this device is bad because it is difficult and its results unpredictable. The writer is always in doubt as to what is going to happen next. (He tries to comfort himself that this same uncertainty will be felt by the reader and this uncertainty will hold the reader's attention and interest.) And inevitably, he wonders with apprehension if he'll ever be able to finish the story—and he usually can't—or if he does finish it, he's forced by the

constraints of his contrivance to resort to a denouement that is very weak and unconvincing.
And the device is also bad because such failures
entrench a negative rather than a positive ap
proach to writing.

4. Don't be constantly interrupting your writing by reading what you've already written;
nibbling at some line or lines. Another form of
the compulsion is to read the whole uncompleted
thing right from the start, changing a word now
and then, or spending a lot of time getting a single
sentence, usually the first one, exactly right.
Such behavior implies doubt in what you've done,
and are doing, and gets you thinking negatively,
and is a call for the muscles to tighten and the
inhibitions to deploy shoulder to shoulder and
to stop any advance. In the case of a novel,
constant rereading is both discouraging and con-
fusing. Long works often rely on the effect of the
whole. By reading a part, rather than the novel
in its entirety, you may be judging too soon.

5. Don't be forever showing partial manuscripts to someone. It implies the need for help.
It also means you're not sure of yourself. You
want those who read your script to say it's terrific, but you're certain they won't. And when
they do exclaim over it, you know it's only because they don't want to hurt you. What best
friend or uncle or grocer would want to be other
than kind?

6. It's not at all unusual, after you finish
writing a book or a story, to be suddenly swamped

by a wave of depression. The excellent aspects of what you've done are submerged and completely lost sight of and the entire work becomes an amorphous, inadequate blur. Here's the antidote for this illusion: Read a published, critically accepted story; then after a few hours start wondering about it in a dubious cynical manner and it will assume an amorphous, inadequate blur. Nothing can stand up before lack of confidence, not even a masterpiece written by someone other than yourself.

7. There is no harm in being influenced or inspired by good writing, but imitation gives you a result which is only an imitation and limits you by the person you're imitating. On the other hand, unlimited freedom is yours when you're yourself, for there is no one pattern to limit you. To be prolific, you must be confident, and originality and freshness is the mark of confidence.

To sum up, before one can sit down and be prolific, one must be able to face one's work in a positive rather than a negative way. Techniques and tricks come after, both in order and in importance, the right frame of mind. The right mental approach is *sine qua non*. With it you can write; without it you can't. Instead of being frozen inactive by the possibilities of failure, you will write. And always bear in mind that no writing that you do is wasted; the real waste, in time and energy, is in what you do not write.

Chapter Two

HOW TO WRITE
PAINLESSLY

A T this point in the book, you impatiently, eagerly wait for revelation, for the skies to split and for the appearance on a cosmic screen of a formula for prolific writing.

It is not enough to be confident, to tell yourself—and especially others—that you're a writer, and a mighty fine one. What's the good of confidence, if when one faces the white sheet in the typewriter, one can't write and the more one can't, the more one can't?

First of all, it is necessary to have something to write about. (The Summer I Visited Yellowstone National Park is something.) Writers, who are not writing, usually have on hand at least the equivalent of The Summer I Visited Yellowstone National Park, but what they don't have are the facts, forgotten sidelights, fresh insights. And they invariably haven't decided exactly what they want to do to the reader: inform him, inform and entertain him, hold him in suspense, make him laugh or cry or both.

So here's the formula: (1) Have something to write about. (2) Have all the material for the particular job that you need. (3) Know what you're trying to accomplish in the way of effect.

Let us say that (1) for example, equals a chase story. Then (2) would include the story's plot. This, in turn, includes not only the story's basic problem, but its characters, complications and resolution. It also includes information about the terrain over which the chase takes place—possibly an area as geographically remote as the North Pole or, if the chase is an illusion, the product of a distraught mind, your material conceivably might come from delving into your own personal emotional makeup. In this instance (3) would undoubtedly have exciting, dramatic entertainment as its purpose. This would therefore restrain you from lengthy *National Geographic* descriptions of the North Pole—if that be the locale of the chase—and it would remind you of the need for the unexpected in the way of complications to rouse a dozing attention; for black moments that would make the reader stick with your hero—even past the reader's bedtime—to see if and how he gets out of the quicksand or if and why he slips from the bad but beautiful woman's embrace.

The writer who is not writing is not following this threefold plan. Assuming that a particular individual is intelligent and literate—if he has the ingredients that are to be used in his story, article, speech, novel or whatever, and has decided upon his objective—he should be able to write.

To find out why writers channel their energies for creating despair rather than copy, it is necessary to consider the positive as against the negative approach to writing.

Confidence is the formula's catalyst. Confidence energizes it. Without confidence, the formula's words have meaning, but are ineffective.

Over a period of many years, I have received numerous calls from writers, some have come and sat down beside my editorial desk, and each in their own way have said, "I'm stuck! For God's sake tell me what to do!"

Confidence is more often mislaid than lost. There are all sorts of things that may cause it to be mislaid; a rejection, editorial or otherwise, or a series of rejections, is the most common cause. What usually happens is that the despondent, worried, apprehensive, defeated-before-he-starts writer attempts to write too soon. He doesn't have all that he needs in the way of material, nor does he know his particular goal. His thoughts are too preoccupied with failure, for him to be able to sit down in a relaxed and tranquil way and patiently do the essential ground work on a script. His thoughts declare the futility of writing. "Most of it is hack work, so why turn it out?" He will rationalize, procrastinate. "I'm looking for just the right treatment," is a dandy, for it's both rationalization and procrastination in one. He will grouse. He may get drunk; he may even stay drunk. The one oppressive certainty in his immediate way of life is that he is not writing.

The beginning writer is also stymied because he starts to write—tries to start, that is—too soon.

The inability to write convinces one, erroneously, that one can't write. All it really means is that one isn't writing. But just as confidence breeds confidence, a lack of confidence grows by accretion into a hard, immovable mass.

In despair, if need be, assume the guise of confidence. Don't grit your teeth—a confident person doesn't have to—as any tension checks the creative flow. Instead, relax, let the ideas come, start working.

There is a bromide and an anecdote that prove all mankind is one. A novelist told me that he was once on the West Coast of Africa and was asked by a native, who was as undressed as a savage, but who spoke with an Oxford accent, "I say, could you tell me where you get your ideas?"

Ideas—and this includes the material of fiction—are not obtainable from some mysterious, external source. They come from inside oneself—and in a really puzzling and wonderful way. Simply stated, writing is merely recording what comes out of you. You're an amanuensis—of all things—nothing more.

To illustrate in a fairly rudimentary way how this works, take the matter of titles. I, as an editor, frequently have to write them. And this, I have found, is the quickest and best way: Write down titles as fast as they occur to you. Write them all down—good and bad, alike. If you keep the critical faculty in abeyance, the titles will continue to come. But the moment you think: "That's no good," you put a kink in the supply line. The mere act of writing—even an inappropriate title—is positive and not inhibiting. It's an act. You're doing something more affirmative than being a statue with a furrowed brow.

Here is how the titles came to me in a particular case; this is the order in which they came to mind. None were rejected. I put them all down:

BELOW THE WATCHING MOUNTAINS
THE MOUNTAINS SAW IT ALL
WITNESSED BY THE MOUNTAINS
TO CATCH A MURDERER
RIFLE BARRELS LIKE RAISED OARS
POSSE
THAT MAKES HIM AN ANIMAL
HUNT FOR A MAN
RIFLES AND MEN
FORGETTING IS A SLOW, STILL THING
FACES OF DEAD MEN

DEAD MEN
TAKE YOUR DEAD FACES AWAY
LINGERING DEAD FACES
LINGERING FACES, DEAD FACES.

It was at this point that I stopped. I knew
LINGERING FACES, DEAD FACES was the
right title for the story; it fitted its mood, and
content, and had a fresh, intriguing quality. Now
the question: Where did this title come from?
I didn't figure it out laboriously. Elements in the
story evoked some of the titles; others arose
through the association of ideas. But at no time
was I thinking hard or straining. The titles just
came and as they came I recorded them. Finally,
the one I liked and could use arrived, or—to put
it another way—I went straight to it along the
stepping stones of association.

Confidence—and the relaxation of confidence—
play an important part in this method for getting
a title. When you sit down and start recording
the titles as fast as they arrive, you know you're
going to get the title you want. It may come after
you've put down just a few titles, or not until
you've put down fifteen—as in the case I noted.
But you can be certain you'll get the title you
want, for the simple, but valid reason that you
always have in the past.

Much the same approach can be used in working out a story. As long as you—and what you
have to offer—are present, you don't need a plot
machine. Let the characters come, the situations,

the complications. And when something arrives that you like, pounce on it with the enthusiasm of the creator—although discoverer more accurately describes your role. There are no rules to limit you; you need only be governed by what you like. This gives you a joyous feeling of freedom. Good writing is simply writing the good things that come to you and they will come to you if you're relaxed and let them come, and accept them when they do come. (Creator or Discoverer may have a status ring, but there is nothing demeaning, actually, in being an Accepter.)

Think of yourself as an experienced, respected movie director whose word is never questioned. You even control the script. In this story that you're working on, what, you ask yourself, would the reader like to see happen at this particular point? (This will always coincide with what you would like to see happen.) Then all you have to do is make it happen. You're the boss.

Even an editor can play this game. We received a story that presented this dramatic situation: A man who has robbed a bank and who is making his getaway through mountainous country meets up with a vacationer and forces him to help him in his escape plan. In the manuscript, as we received it, the vacationer's identity was not pinned down. He was a vacationer, nothing more. But he had a cynical, offhand manner. It was this characteristic, I'm sure, that gave me the idea. Instead of this man being a vacationer, wouldn't it be far more intriguing, I thought, if he were a confidence man, laying low in the mountains because the heat's on. His cynical, patronizing manner would then fit him better, make more sense. What fun to have the confidence man—who lives by his wit—pitted against the holdup man who gets his loot in a more forceful, physical way. The reader would desperately want to know what is going to happen. There's the holdup man with his gun trained on the confidence man, the gun a symbol of the man's whole approach to his trade and life. And all the while, his counterpart—the confidence man—is at work in his quiet, poised, condescending way not only to outwit his opponent, but to get possession of the money the man had so considerately withdrawn from a bank.

Always bear in mind that the characters, the scenes, the props—everything—are in your hands. You must above all else be confident you can handle the job. It's a fact that the capable person without confidence is not equal to the not-quite-so-capable person with confidence.

Remember, when you're doing a scene that the possibilities for dialogue and action are infinite. As soon as you know where you want the scene to go, the ground it's to cover, let the characters take over and do the scene for you. Let's say a timid fellow has come to ask his girl for a date, but he's delighted to find that she's not home and that he'll therefore get out of asking her. After talking to her kid brother for awhile, he makes his escape before the girl has a chance to return. A thousand writers would do this scene in a thousand different ways. There is no one way that it need be done. If the thousand writers are competent, the thousand scenes they do will have one thing in common: every word, every movement will ring true and the scene, as a consequence, will be alive and genuine.

You may not write the scene the way you want it, the first time. And here is the rule to follow on first drafts: do the best you can do, but no better. The rule on any draft: do the best you can do, but no better. If you attempt the impossible—a perfect script—you won't do the possible, a salable one. You may not even do a script.

It is necessary to do the best you can do in the first draft, for two very good reasons. If you're doing a careless, indifferent job—telling yourself that good writing is rewriting and that you'll take care of everything in the rewrite—you will be reluctant to face the rewrite. And if you've done a bad enough draft, an entire new start—rather than a rewrite—may be required.

But in the first draft you must be careful not to be overly critical. Having all the material you need and knowing your objective, get the draft down on paper in white heat. Don't write a sentence and then read it to determine if it is worthy of your byline or to ponder what such and such an editor will think when he reads it. And don't continue thus to write and read and ponder, cross out and insert; search the thesaurus for just the right word, (Why get the "right" word, when in the next draft the sentence of which it is a part may be deleted?); check the dictionary for spelling or the telephone book for a name for one of your characters; go out to the kitchen and read a passage to your wife for approval and, before she says a critical word, interpret the expression on her face as derogatory or at least dubious and turn martyr-sullen and heroically-tragic and refuse to believe her when she vehemently declares, "But I love it! I just love it! You didn't give me a chance to tell you that I love it!" and, because you still don't believe her, you shuffle to your bedroom and lie down and tell the ceiling that you're done writing for the day—perhaps for ever.

The moral, then, is to do the first draft, the whole first draft. The next step is evaluation, editing, rewriting. (You're better off not showing it to your wife, even at this stage; she may say something, or not say something—and either may be equally disastrous.)

To approach your second draft with apprehension is a mistake. It's much better to feel that you're going to make the original version even better than it is, and though this may possibly take some time, it will be time spent interestingly and enjoyably.

If you go at your second draft with fear and reluctance, you will tend to work more slowly than you should. You'll find yourself held in immobility by a word, or a phrase, or a sentence. And the only way you can break free is by finding the perfect, the unassailable word, phrase or sentence. Aside from the crawling pace of this approach, it is a generator of doubts and fears. Because the iota that you're hovering over is dubious, you begin to wonder—and you have the time to wonder—if the whole thing hasn't been one big mistake.

The best approach is to go through the first draft as quickly as you can read, editing—and editing quickly—as you go. Having gone through the entire script in this way, repeat the process again and again—and again, if you are still finding ways in which to improve it. In the first speedy run through, if you question a passage for some reason, for the sake of speed it is better to merely put a question mark in the margin than to attempt to take care of the problem at this point.

Finally, you will reach a stage in the revision when it is all right for you to move more slowly. Now, if need be, you may heft one word and then another and decide between them. You may deal with words now, because the whole with which you are so terribly familiar, by repetition and long association, has taken on the character of a meaningless blur. Don't let this disturb you. You may be certain that whoever reads the script for the first time will find it fresh and meaningful, and that if you were to put it aside for a time and then come back to it, it will be so good that it will be hard for you to believe that you wrote it—will actually appear not to have been written by you at all, but by some other very good writer, one who certainly bears watching.

If you're going to be a writer in a complete sense—also a prolific one—you won't have 9 to 5 hours; you'll be a writer at all times, at the typewriter or away from it. When you're not writing, you'll be observing and absorbing. If you don't do this, you may come to the sudden realization that your apperceptive storehouse contains only the harvests of your childhood. You'll be like the senile individual who is always telling the same story to the same people. You won't have a wealth of material from which to draw.

Observation requires a relaxed, unhurried frame of mind. You have to be able to look at something, anything, long enough to experience it in a way that you have never experienced it before —and perhaps no one else has—or not exactly in your individual way. Because this is enjoyable and resembles loafing, somewhat, it may, as a consequence, be suspect. One writer, for example, had this to say; it's verbatim from a tape recorder: "It's difficult for me to relax when I'm working because when I do, I have the feeling I'm not working hard enough. I feel better when I hammer my forehead with my fist for an idea or pace around my typewriter or yank false starts out, crumple 'em in a ball, and throw 'em in the wastebasket. This sort of thing makes me feel as if I'm accomplishing something. You know? Another thing, the atmosphere's quieter when I'm relaxed, in a way you have to get used to, I guess. And time feels different, seems to be going slower and I seem to be wasting more of it. When I *have* relaxed, I know I've accomplished more. And it's been pleasanter working that way. Much pleasanter. But when something's pleasant, it's not like work and I feel guilty for not doing what seems like work."

Observation is also related to curiosity and interest and the positive, confident approach to writing. It's the defeated who are blasé, indifferent and unreceptive. They can't write, certainly not prolifically, nor can they know the pleasure of operating with a minimum of friction.

It is, of course, not enough to be a prolific writer, to have few if any blocks in the creative supply lines. It is also of vital importance that one be a discerning writer. This is a matter of personality. What a writer reads and thinks and feels, everything that shapes him as an individual will determine what he writes and the judgment and taste that will help him decide his writing's ultimate form. And though it is a relatively simple thing to teach one a procedure that will make the continuous production of copy possible, it is a bit more difficult to shape a person benignly in order that his copy be improved; this worthwhile undertaking, incidentally, is not a part of this book's objective.

Chapter Three

HOW TO MAKE WRITING
COME ALIVE

THE facility for turning out copy equals the belief that one has in oneself.

Here's a quote from a diary that says pretty much the same thing: "I put off writing because I don't like to write, and I don't like to write because I don't think I write well enough to sell." Obviously, the tortured writer who made this confession to his diary suffered frustration by not writing, but this he preferred to facing possible rejection.

Thought of failure, however, doesn't enter the mind of the prolific writer. He writes. His energy is not divided between writing and indecision. A correlation definitely exists between production and a forthright, positive approach.

And when you believe in yourself, in your potential and your performance, the result is not only more writing, but better writing. Your writing doesn't waver uncertainly, but moves with an air of authority which is, of course, the reflection of your own confidence.

What is more, this sureness, and this faith in oneself, makes an individual style possible, for style is a true reflection of oneself. It's not difficult to mimic a style. After reading a chapter of Somerset Maugham—a writer I've selected arbitrarily—it is easy to then sit down and write a page that has the rhythm and pace and word choice of Somerset Maugham. It is more important to let your own individuality come through; your writing shouldn't be a masquerade; it should be you.

And when you can be yourself—that is, when you're sold on your own merits—you're bound to feel a joyous freedom that's like the release of religious conversion. You too have seen the light. Not only can you write as you please—the sort of thing, in short, that you would like to read—but you can allow yourself to come up with fresh angles. To be original, aside from having the requisite talent, it is essential that one be relaxed and uninhibited.

After being an editor for years, the pattern that unacceptable material takes is not only clear to me, but I know it is inviolate. The editor does not always have time, as the printed rejection slips invariably state, to give a detailed analysis of why a script failed. Instead, I, for one, try to illumine what is wrong by a word or phrase that goes straight as a beam of light to the manuscript's shortcomings.

"Doesn't come alive." "Doesn't ring true." "Not plausible." "Lacks sense of reality." "Story's too thin"—and to lighten the blow—"for us," the implication being that it might not be too thin for someone else. "Plot's too familiar." "Situation's been overdone." (If a husband's going to kill his wife or vice versa, something new—and this means more than just a change of locale or murder weapon—has to be added.)

These comments are invariably necessary because the writer did not believe, in a very real sense, in what he was writing. And for a writer to believe in what he is writing, he must be free of doubts about himself.

The writer must not only believe in his story as a whole, but in all the components that make it up. The characters, the story's basic problem, complications, dialogue, exposition—everything in the story—must ring true; every word, even the smallest action, must be right, must be felt and be believed.

This may appear at first to make being prolific impossible. Actually just the opposite is true: you have much more to write about when you make things come alive—and, the writing is easier.

To write a great deal about a little is not advocating verbosity or "padding." There's a great difference between saying something quite simple at great length, and in delving and probing and coming up with new insights and new information. There is also the matter of conveying emotion—which good fiction must do—which flows naturally and effortlessly when the writer himself feels the emotion he wants the reader to experience.

When you have a sense of reality as a criterion of what you should write and by which your writing should be judged, you are able to proceed with more certainty. You have something very definite and unchanging at which to aim.

This does not mean that reality should be your objective, but a sense of reality, and there's a great and important difference between the two. Fiction must seem real, but have many qualities not present in simple fact. In a movie that lasts not even two hours, you may witness a cavalcade that spans a few generations and not be aware of this discrepancy in time. In fiction, you may be cleansed by tragedy, enobled by character, enriched by the illumination of some aspect of life. There is, consequently, an incalculable difference between fiction and newspaper writing—objective statement of fact. In works of fiction much is stated as though it were fact, but the reader gains much more than mere information.

To achieve this semblance of reality, you must understand the basic elements that are invariably a part of reality. Once you know what

these elements are—and this is a simple matter—
and develop an intuitive feeling for them—which
is not as simple or as easy—you can manufacture,
endlessly, what will pass for reality. Writers who
must depend on relating what has happened to
them, thinly disguised in order to make fiction
of it, are quite obviously restrained and limited.

Here are some of reality's ingredients, certainly
ones a writer can not ignore. Conflict—reality is
charged with it. Take the incidents in a day—
any day, and the day of any individual—and you'll
find varying degrees of conflict. When you wake
up in the morning, you may very likely engage
in a duel. One part of you says, "Remember, you
got hell yesterday for being late to work," and
a more lovable aspect of yourself answers lan-
guorously, "Couple more minutes in bed, that's
all, and I'll be up." But you take more than a
couple more minutes, which may mean that you
gulp a cup of coffee on the run, which leads not
only to some conflict with the terribly hot coffee,
but to a monologue by your wife which in essence
points out that families that have a leisurely
breakfast together are more likely to stay together. You slam the door on the monologue, but
not on conflict, for sure enough the car won't
start. It's that damned, so-called automatic choke
again. But as luck will have it, the fellow across
the street is just leaving for work and you get
a lift with him. There should be no conflict now,
for this fellow's a "sweet guy"—friendly, well-
adjusted, active in PTA. You can't stand him.

You're sure you're superior to him, because you're not well-adjusted, which means you have more awareness of the stinking nature of the world in which man finds himself. You don't want to get too friendly with this guy and get involved with him socially. You therefore find yourself saying such things as, "What do you mean it's a fine day? What's fine about it?" and "You're a Republican, aren't you? Why? Because your old man was one? I don't know of a better reason *you* could have for being a Republican." And so it goes, conflict, conflict, conflict the whole live-long day.

Life, or reality, is also filled with the unexpected. In fiction, it is known as a complication. The unexpected return of the husband—that sort of thing. But in addition to such untoward vital occurrences, reality is made up of—is riddled with—things happening in not quite the expected way. The guest is to arrive by plane; well, he comes by car, or he comes by plane, but his visit is postponed by a month, or he comes by plane and the plane doesn't make it and, therefore, neither does he. Or, he is supposed to come for dinner, but he breaks his leg between living room and dining room and stays on and on. (Some author or other, I do believe, has used this very complication.)

It is conceivable that in real life a young man may decide to marry a girl, he may forthwith propose to her, and she may as forthwith accept and the wedding may take place on the scheduled June date. This, however, is not the normal or the average reality—that everything should work out precisely as planned. And in a story, this pat, rapid-fire progression—decision to marry, proposal, wedding—is not only dull, but it is not satisfying. Reality, remember, is saturated with conflict or the promise of it. (The promise of conflict is sometimes as good as conflict.) There is obviously not enough conflict, or a semblance of genuineness, in a story that proceeds in a straight line to its conclusion. It therefore shouldn't be plotted in that way.

Another characteristic of reality is its constancy. If an individual in real life has a big nose, it's big all the time—at home and at work, night and day, and it has been big in the past and it continues to be in the present. So if you have a character in a story whose nose is more than apparent, it is impossible to merely mention this olfactory fact when the character is introduced and then forget it. (Cf., *Cyrano* by Edmond Rostand.) Moreover, if the character is real to the writer, he has a strong visual reality, and it should therefore be impossible for the writer to forget that nose, and that nose may very well dictate—figuratively, of course—what its owner says, and thinks, and the course that the plot is going to take.

Character tags are all right because they are founded in reality. Men do have big noses. Or one will introduce almost everything he says with the phrase "funny thing," even ludicrously when what is said is not funny at all. ("Funny thing, I just saw him at lunch and he goes and falls down dead of a heart attack.") Or the salient aspect of the man's secretary will be that she douses her cigarette butts in the cold, Dixie cup dregs of her coffee. Everyone—because everyone has individuality of sorts—can be pinned down with a tag. The elevator man hums *Meet Me in St. Louis, Louie,* when going up as well as when going down. And perhaps the thought of one of his regular passengers is invariably, "Why that particular song? It's wishful thinking. He wants to move horizontally to St. Louis, instead of up and down to nowhere." Joe is dour; his favorite expression, "Everything has its price tag." And when Frank comes to call in the evening, he starts yawning mightily at 9:30; you can set your watch by it. The examples are infinite.

But a simple character tag doesn't make a character. It may do no more than identify him. (In the old pulp story, a tag would frequently be used instead of the person's name: Big Belly, or Sharp Clothes or Mr. Or-else. And in the early days of radio, on dramatic shows, the characters were in part chosen by voice so that each would be distinguishable from the other. And so, one script might have a heavily brogued Irishman, a Chinese houseboy, a coloratura heroine, a lisping villain and a flighty-voiced mother.)

One reason for the importance of characterization is that it brings your story closer to reality and therefore to complete credibility. In real life, people are always more than just a name plus a skimpy description. Your story has more chance to ring true if it is inhabited by multi-dimensional characters. And only if a character is real to you, can you make him come alive on paper. He should be there in your imagination, seen through scrim perhaps, but seen. It is he who does the talking and the acting, and all you are is his Boswell. His speech is right, for it is coming straight from his mouth, and there you are if he gets out of line to write him right back into character.

When characters are delineated in this way, it is not necessary to hang a tag on a character in order to create a character. The tags will come of themselves, in much the same way that what a character says and does will come from his make-up and not from that of the writer. And that characters really live in a realistic sense, is certainly more desirable than that their existence hinges on blowing their nose raucously, or pulling on their right earlobe when an idea of inspirational proportions occurs to them, or being in the habit of losing door keys.

The writer's belief in his characters must be preceded by his belief in himself. He must never feel that characterization is beyond him, just as he should never proclaim—and if he does it once, he'll find it so pleasureable that he'll do it repeatedly—that he's not good at plotting, or that he has trouble with his women (in writing), or that his talent is for nothing over 5,000 words in length, and so on and so on.

This confidence that a writer must feel is also

definitely related to the detail that he uses in
his writing, and which is extremely important
in evoking the illusion of reality. First of all, the
detail of reality is very specific. There's the expression of being as familiar with something as
with the palm of one's hand. But if you look at
the palm of your hand—one rarely does—you'll
be surprised by the detail of its terrain that you
had never observed before—topographical ex-
tremes, lines, color, texture, even size.

This shouldn't give you the idea that your
story should be clogged with detail. Your job is
primarily the job of telling a story; the details,
the descriptions, should help the story, not impede
it. When the murderer rings the door bell and the
housewife answers, the reader might very well be
impatient, if not annoyed, should two pages be
devoted to the details making up the reality of
the housecoat that the woman is wearing.

What the writer, obviously, must snatch from
the innumerable details of reality is its essence,
its universality, and this will make his writing
come alive and be convincing. There is a considerable difference, for example, between: They
were always quarreling. And: Their disagreements
were the comfortable conflict of an old marriage.
One difference is that the second statement says
much more than the first, and another difference
is that it contains, in addition to fact, an essential,
recognizable truth.

Remember, there is no rule against your using

any pertinent detail that you like. Remember, you have your choice at all times of infinite possibilities.

Here's a selection from an issue of the magazine I edited that contains telling, fresh detail: "Beaufort sighed and walked out of the station house that smelled like a wet stale cigar. It was a sultry day, one which had lost its sunlight and become the color of a dove." Such imaginative detail is not to be confused with fancy writing that is not imaginative, but merely purple—and is so designated on a rejection slip. Fancy writing is not genuine, because the writer and his terrible determination to be awfully good intrudes and destroys all illusion of reality. You may say: Orpheus would not come, would not come, and outside his window was the eternal night. But you're closer to reality with: He lay awake; far, far off, on his auditory horizon, there was the barking of a dog.

If you're going to be a prolific writer, and that means one who can deftly, unerringly create the illusion of reality, at no point in any story on which you're working should you forget what has gone before. By this constant remembrance of things past, your belief and the reader's belief in the reality of what you have written is reinforced.

When you say ". . . walked out of the station house that smelled like a wet stale cigar," you've committed yourself to the sort of station house it is. The only way you can change that station

house from being one that smells like a wet stale
cigar is by having it torn down in the course of
the story and having a new and fragrant station
house erected. But even in the act of tearing it
down, you're confirming that it is a smelly structure and worthy of being torn down.

So it is with any specific detail that you put in
your story. Once it's down on paper, it's real,
genuine, and it cannot be forgotten or ignored.
You, for example, just can't say that a character
is physically big, but small spiritually and then
forget your appraisal of that individual. You can't
say a torrential rain is in progress and then forget
that rain is falling or that it is torrential. If your
locale is India, it remains India in every sentence
you write.

You can't even permit the content of a bit of
dialogue to disappear as though it had never been;
its existence must continue. And when the author
comes back to the dialogue in some way, the
author is proving to the reader that he believes
in it. And by affirming its reality in this way, he
gives it reality. Reality, true reality, has a past
as well as a present.

Here's an example. A salesman comes into an
office and tries to make a sale. In the course of
his pitch, he tells this joke: A businessman was
told to be cheerful, because things could be worse.
So he was cheerful and sure enough, things were
worse. Later that day, the man to whom this
joke was told received a phone call from his wife
who informed him that she had a bad headache

because the children were acting up more so than usual. To help her forget her headache, the man found himself telling her the joke the salesman told him that morning. A month later, he again thinks of the joke while reading an account of an air crash in which the salesman was killed who had told the joke to him. This is the natural reiteration of reality. Or say you have a character named John who has just come to New York from Indiana, from a small town in Indiana. That he has just made the transition from hamlet to metropolis, will continually be in evidence. He may get lost, he may be homesick, he may talk to someone whom he comes upon in a car with an Indiana license plate. A writer, in short, simply cannot say John came to New York from Indiana and then lose sight of the fact that John came to New York from Indiana.

So not only is everything that is written in a story concrete, specific, stated with authority, and believed in, but it has a continuing reality. A similar reality exists prior to the writing of the story—that is, during the course of its being plotted. Say you start with a character. To be a character, a character must have a dominant trait. The trait must always be present in your thinking, the trait and all the details that give it individuality. It will do your plotting for you. Such a person must act in a certain way in a particular situation, and when he acts in this way, this might happen or that might happen. Even a mannerism of one of your characters might prove valuable in the development of the plot. Or so might a particular aspect of the locale. And just as you must believe in all the elements of your story when you're writing it, so too must it seem alive and real to you after you've figured it out. It has to ring true and be interesting. You should be able to tell the story to someone as though it were the truth, and hold and convince your audience. To actually do this is not advisable, for writers are usually heavy-tongued and terribly sensitive and so having told the story badly, they may, before they're through, be convinced that it is utterly worthless and not to be written.

A confident hold on the reality of a script breathes life into it. So many scripts which we received and which we had to reject did not come alive and therefore did not ring true. We frequently received letters in which a proposed story was summarized, after which we were asked if we would be interested in seeing this story in a finished form. And these summaries were, invariably, the barest of outlines. We, of course, had to answer, "In our opinion, it's impossible to appraise a story in summary form; we have to see what you can do with it." And "what you can do with it," means "if you can make it live."

I've said that the reality of fiction resembles reality and partakes of its truth and soars above plain fact. In the conventional short story, there is a big central problem that must be resolved by the action of its characters. Day to day reality, as everyone knows, usually doesn't have such a big problem, with complications and denouement; it usually has many problems that stay right with one with the persistence of gnats and have no resolution with all loose ends tied in a neat bow.

Of course, as in fiction, a real life detective may look down at a lifeless body and be confronted with the whodunit problem. (And the body, moreover, may be that of an attractive blonde.) But the detective may get a confession so fast that there's no story, or the murder may never be solved, or it may be solved after forty-two years and make a paragraph in the paper as an oddity.

Stories must have a lot more direction and Aristotleian unity than this. Commercial fiction, really commercial fiction, requires a well-rounded plot; a slice of life is not enough; or a character study; or a mood piece; or something so obscure that it may possibly be profound.

Our slush pile has been high with scripts that go on and on for five pages or more without a story being apparent, simply because there's no problem around. It's difficult for the writers of such stories to be prolific—and successful—because they don't know what a short story requires of them. Because they haven't taken care of that third step—knowing precisely what their objective is—they meander. They may write interestingly, but there is no apparent point or goal to what they have written. Everything must contribute to what the writer is out to achieve. Everything must have that air of certainty that the writer should feel about his story. Paddy Chayefsky in writing of *Marty* said, "I tried to write the dialogue as if it had been wire-tapped. I tried to envision the scenes as if a camera had been focused upon the unsuspecting characters and had caught them in an untouched moment of life."* The essence of the show, he had decided, was its "literal reality."

Deep down a writer may know he has a weak story on his hands. What he should do is try and strengthen it, or if that doesn't work he should throw the story out when it's in the plotting stage, and start from scratch. Though this isn't in the same league with infanticide as practiced by the ancient Greeks (destroying unfit infants by abandoning them on a mountainside), some writers emote as though it were. And just as color or a wide screen or drum beating can't make an essentially bad movie one whit better, an odd treatment isn't going to improve a weak, inferior story. Another form of obscurity that a writer may use when he feels his story is limping and needs assistance is to withhold certain information, about the protagonist or about what is going on, to pique the reader's curiosity and, of course, that all-important curiosity: an editorial office's first reader. Or the writer with a poor story may insist that it is not poor, but different, and therefore better than the stories

---

* From *Television Plays,* copyright © 1955 by Paddy Chayefsky; Reprinted by permission of Simon and Schuster, Inc.

that are being published. A "different" story is
fine if it is actually an improvement on those
usually done, but if it is not as good—obviously,
far from being as good—its difference has been
a liability. (It is not easy to put across a taut
domestic drama in which the participants are
earthworms, living at the time of the Second
Crusade.)

All these forms of obscurity are usually the
result of the writer's uncertainty; sometimes, of
course, it may simply be a case of his being
muddled, but this, too, may stem from uncertainty. He is afraid of a clear, simple statement; in fact, he may be terrified of it. Feeling
unsure of himself, he wants what he does to be
terribly impressive. And yet, if one is to create
an illusion of reality, it is best done simply and
with clarity.

A writer should make use of any special knowledge that he may have. If he lives among the
natives of Equatorial Africa or those of Montana, it would be more than an oversight if some
of his copy did not make use of the background
he has at hand. Details from little written about
areas tend to give the impression the author knows
what he is talking about—and this is always
advisible. There is this admonition: the writer
in Equatorial Africa may dry-wash his hands
avariciously over his font of virginal material,
whereas the one in Montana may not appreciate
the material around him (since it's not quite as
obviously different as that in Equatorial Africa).

And the time to make the most of fresh material is when you first come upon it. That's when it's most novel; that's when you can be excited about it. Let a month go by and teeth filed to points or a breakfast of steak and hash browned potatoes, or the little hillbilly woman who has an electric refrigerator but no electricity—and keeps clothes in the refrigerator and her food in a spring— will seem as commonplace as the telephone and coffee and doughnuts.

In this connection, there's that admonitory cliché: "Write only what you know." The idea being that if you're in Equatorial Africa, you're foolish to be writing about East Harlem which you know only by hearsay. You can certainly write with more confidence about the former and, of course, if you can't write with confidence, it's not likely that you will be writing well or much. It isn't that you need to have an encyclopedic quantity of information, but what you need more than information is the "feel" of a place and its people. And you need this primarily because it makes it possible for you to write with authority —which is the same as writing with confidence.

A writer traveled all over South America, preparatory to writing a magazine serial with a South American background. He went into areas of the Mato Grosso where no white man had ever been before, went all around the Horn, but when he sat down to write, he found he didn't have all the information he needed and it was therefore necessary for him to do further research in the library. But now these book-facts had a meaning for him that they couldn't possibly have had before he'd made the trip.

And this writer told me that the trip had made it possible for him to pick out the pertinent and telling detail. It is such details that give genuineness to your writing. If you have a teenager say, as I heard one say, "I get a blast out of reading books," it rings true. And it has more character in it than a long paragraph filled with "cool man, cool," and other stereotype beat talk. You believe a fictional mailman's saying, "I'm sure snowed under this morning," more readily than if he'd said, "I've certainly got a lot of mail to deliver." Or, to take another example, if one of the characters in your story should happen to be cleaning a gun, it would not be at all advisable to stop your story by the insertion of a technical treatise lifted from Stoeger's gun catalogue, but a special fact or two—perhaps the number of oil that he is using, if oil is used—might make the reader believe in the gun-cleaning sequence.

Though the genuine feel of a story stems from facts, imagination should not be bound by facts, but only by the "facts" it creates. More important to the writer than knowing what a character actually did is the knowledge of what he might do. For what he really did is limited, obviously, by what he really did; what he might do, is unlimited.

It is now in order to give this command: Don't be afraid to use your imagination, and in straying from factual reality, create a new reality in which you believe and in which the reader will believe.

We frequently find letters, accompanying manuscripts, which inform us that the story really happened and that the author has merely changed the names of the real people involved and has tampered with the facts just a little. The implication is that such a story is the most desirable. That a writer, let us say, gave a lift in his car to a man who had just escaped from an asylum for the criminally insane might very well make it difficult for him to write a good story making use of this situation. "The way it really happened" will always be getting in the way. What is wanted is not "the way it really happened," but the way it might happen most entertainingly. In a case like this, the writer has a better chance of doing a good job, if he doesn't draw on his experience immediately, but allows a considerable interval of time to elapse during which his experience can dissolve and merge with all his other experiences. This will give it a chance to develop in the manner of legends and tall stories; the fish that got away needs only time to become a better, and bigger, specimen.

The writer, in short, if he is to be prolific must be able to blend finite experience with infinite imagination.

Chapter Four

HOW TO WRITE PROLIFICALLY
IN YOUR SPARE TIME

WRITERS — somehow — are especially conscious of time. When they're writing well, days are only minutes long. They may then get melodramatic and proclaim that they're racing Death to get their next piece of work done—even if it's nothing more than a filler on modern plastics.

A writer told me that he works best when he ignores time, by regarding it as a continuous stream—instead of the bits into which it is hacked by the clock and the calendar. He then doesn't feel its pressure only its laving calm.

But this is not an indulgence for the individual who must work all day, and, if he is to write, must do it in his spare time. Spare time consists in such cases of time in the evening and/or night and on week ends. This is what is usually meant by spare time. But I say to you, don't overlook spare time on your job, or when you brush your teeth, or when you lie awake at night and can't sleep.

Your job, no matter what its nature, offers you spare time. Justify using it, for your personal writing ends, by assuring your conscience that one's employer deserves to be a patron of the arts. Some clever, shrewd, facile, ambitious editors that I have known have found enough free moments in the office to write, actually write, stories, articles, big hunks of novels. So if you're a barber, don't throw away slack afternoons by leafing lazily through the girly magazines that are around for the customers. Or if you're a musician in the pit of a loud musical, don't spend the quiet, non-musical interludes reading; put your instrument to one side and write. Or if you're a commuter and your train stops between stations, for some reason known only to trains, and sits and sits, as such trains so often do, write.

Because of all these on-the-job opportunities, if you're to be a prolific spare-time writer, spare time must be redefined. It is more than the conventional after-dinner and week-end hours; *it is any time that can be utilized*. This may sound terribly Spartan and arduous. But whether it does or not depends on how much you want to write, how much you really want to, how much writing means to you.

James Thurber was a full-time, professional writer—as you all know—but his use of spare time is significant for the spare-time writer.

"I never quite know when I'm not writing," Thurber once said. "Sometimes my wife comes up to me at a party and says, 'Dammit, Thurber, stop writing.' She usually catches me in the middle of a paragraph. Or my daughter will look up from the dinner table and ask, 'Is he sick?' 'No,' my wife says, 'he's writing something.' "

That you do what Thurber did is very important if you're going to be more than just a dilettante. If you're an elevator operator, for example, you can hardly set up a typewriter beside your up-and-down control. But you can do a lot of work in your head, especially when you're on the ground floor waiting for the car to fill up and for the starter to send you on your way. You can plot. You can observe the people who enter your elevator. A meticulous mustache may enter jauntily. Notice clothing. Wonder if the girl with the empty expression really has something in her mind, and what it might possibly be. Listen to speech. See it as dialogue on a page. Note its rhythm; its structure.

No matter what your job, you can—to lesser or greater degree—do this kind of writing work. A cop on a stake-out, a dentist prying out a recalcitrant tooth, a strip tease promenading and removing, a politician smiling and shaking hands.

All this is very important spare time work, for the spare time writer. It readies him for the time when he sits down at the typewriter to write, for at that time, if he is to be prolific, he must write and do nothing else. That is not the time to wonder and figure and ponder, for if this time is used in this way nothing will be produced but discouragement and futility.

But let us say that you've come home from a hard day at the office. Let us also assume that this is an evening that you've decided to work. Perhaps what made it a hard day at the office brought you around to that decision. Your work is routine, uncreative, unsatisfying. You therefore want to express yourself. And you also daydream: you've written a runaway bestseller; you're wealthy; you're a name worthy of being dropped.

Remember how tired you are, and remember your dream. You rush through dinner, because you only have a couple of hours before you'll have to brush your teeth and get to bed, so that you'll be bright and alert the next day for that job of yours that you hate.

You go into the bedroom where your typewriter squats stolidly under its cover. You take off the cover. It's as if you've seen that typewriter for the first time. Why, the thing's a solid lump of unfeeling metal. To spend two hours with it is suddenly abhorrent.

You start telling yourself interesting things. An artist, you remind yourself, doesn't create on order, doesn't hand ultimatums to his soul. How could you possibly have forgotten that? Besides you're tired. If you wrote, it would just be drivel. And this isn't just an excuse to get out of writing; it's just plain common sense. And after a hard day, didn't he deserve a little recreation. God, he didn't want his whole life to be work, work, work and nothing but work. He might drop dead next week—after all he was in the fatal forties—and look at all that he would have missed. For what? He might as well go out and watch TV. That's right, he remembers, there's a very good show on. It'd be a shame to miss it; he might get a lot of ideas from it. It was important to keep up with the good things that were being done.

Then as he marches out to the TV set which his wife is watching without any feelings of guilt —looking as if Euphoria is her middle name—he gets good and sore. Why did he have to give all those excuses to himself, just to go out and watch a simple, little TV show? He hadn't committed a crime by not sitting down there and writing. He didn't have to write. He had to go to work in the morning, but damned if he had to write when he was dead tired and besides . . .

At this point, his wife whom he really loves asks, without lifting her eyes from the TV set, "How'd the writing go, dear? Are you all done?"

So what else can he say, but, "Yeah, yeah, I'm all done?" And by done, he means through, finished, washed-up.

To be prolific in your spare time, you must go

about the whole matter in a somewhat different way.

In order to be fair, let's take the same individual: tired, disgusted with his job, determined to create. What is important is that there be a break—especially a psychological one—between his job and his session at the typewriter.

A long, hot shower goes a long way to remove the grime of the job. Make a ritual of it, a ritual of purification. Many like to include a sacramental cocktail as part of the deal. One—or maybe two—drinks are all that the liturgy allows. Remember that the bulk of the service is to be a sober wrestling with your typewriter.

This liquid break—of shower and cocktail—should give you the feeling that you're starting a new day joyously, instead of ending one miserably. And if you still have an inclination to do something other than write, like watch TV, recall that once you get started, writing is much more enjoyable than a somnolent, guilty viewing of something that is television-terrible.

Hemingway had a method of getting started at the typewriter that may be of value to you. This applies to a piece of work already begun. Whenever you finish for the day or night, stop while you're going along at a fast clip and with enthusiasm, stop in the middle of a paragraph, even before the completion of a particular sentence. It is much easier to take up from such a point, than from a solid block of writing complete in every respect.

So you get started. It's important now not to feel the pressure of time. Writing at top speed is fine, but you mustn't feel pursued. You mustn't start paying attention to those thoughts, flowing along under your writing thoughts, that you haven't much time, and that what you get done in the little time that you have will be negligible. Once the clock starts chasing you, all sorts of glands let go to protect you as an organism. But the final result is a harried, unhappy individual. And if you're going to be prolific, as a spare-time writer, you have to pace yourself so that you're happy while working, so that you, as a consequence, can work night, after night, after night— and on week ends, too. And do it for years, even for decades.

There are sly ways of getting around this need for a feeling of accomplishment, even though the period of your work is no more than an hour or two in duration. There are writers who specialize in fairly short short stories, ones that they can do at a sitting. But if you're working on, let us say, a novel—even a very long novel—break it up for the sake of your psyche into segments or scenes that you can write in an evening. Moving your hero, for example, from the basement where he is growing mushrooms to the kitchen where he quaffs a can of beer is a good evening's work and should make you quite pleased with yourself.

When engaged on a long book, refrain from thinking, "My God, I've hardly done anything. And I've got so much more to do. The trouble is,

I don't have enough time. An hour here, and an hour there, it's just no good. This spare-time writing is for the birds . . ."

Do one little chore at a time. And, if you must, tell yourself that big oaks from little acorns grow. And more important is this fact: if you're working and writing in your spare time, you don't have the economic pressure of the full-time writer. What you write doesn't have to sell. And what's more, you may write whatever you please and don't have to write the sort of thing that may actually repel you. So just remember, when you start griping to yourself and to others, that spare-time writing has its advantages, too.

Perhaps one reason that your spare time is inadequate is that you're fastidious. Just as the full-time writer often demands that the conditions of his environment be absolutely perfect, the spare-time writer—in his spare time, of course—carries on in an equally temperamental fashion.

Abraham Lincoln walking miles to school and doing his homework by firelight is still thrown up to students who have their own car and good reading lamps, but get bad grades just the same. So the spare-time writer, complaining bitterly about the conditions under which he must write, should take a look at what other writers have accomplished in far from ideal settings.

Jane Austen, history tells us, wrote in the midst of family conversations. William Faulkner wrote SANCTUARY, a terrific popular success, in the boiler room of a power plant in which he was employed. He worked on the book between twelve midnight and four in the morning. He wrote it on a table improvised out of a turned-over wheelbarrow, while a dynamo near by made a steady, humming noise. Trollope, a notably prolific writer, worked in a post office, and so he did his writing before he went to work, and on his way to work, in trains and on horseback. His mother was no slouch either. Trollope in his autobiography had this to say of her writing prowess: "She was at her writing table at four in the morning, and had finished her work before the world had begun to be aroused . . . She continued writing up to 1856, when she was seventy-six years old, and had at that time produced one hundred and fourteen volumes, of which the first was not written till she was past fifty . . . Her career offers encouragement to those who have not begun early in life, but are still anxious to do something before they depart hence."

And let us not overlook Abraham Lincoln, in this connection; he might very well be thrown up to complaining writers—as he is to non-exemplary students. He wrote what he called his "little speech" under trying circumstances. His son Tad was gravely ill; the Civil War was being fought. He wrote a hurried first draft, using both pencil and ink, using both—no doubt—because pencil points always seem to break when you're in a rush, and pens, maniacally, run out of ink. But that "little speech" of Lincoln's, its 263 words, is known, with reverence and respect, as The Gettysburg Address.

By now the point must be fairly clear, and emphasized, that the spare-time writer—especially the spare-time writer—must not be overly fussy. He must not pamper himself. Granted, his time is limited. Why, then, limit it further by making special demands of it?

A writer told me how he made use of two hours traveling time every day on the New York, New Haven and Hartford Railroad.

"It was like a race," he said. "That on your mark, get set, go, business. When I got on the train in the morning, I knew in a general way what writing ground I was going to cover. And before the other passengers could unfold their newspapers, I was writing away. I didn't let up either until we pulled into Grand Central . . ."

He always picked a seat in the middle of the train, because he'd heard that there were less vibrations there and his writing, as a consequence, would be more legible.

There was always the danger that he would sit down beside someone who talked, or who wanted to talk. He fought this sort of individual with reticence. And the dedicated, almost furious, way he went at his writing hinted to the talkative one beside him that this was something he must do.

The movement of the train and its noises, he found soothing rather than disturbing. The pattern of swaying and jerks and sounds, repeated in a kind of endless monotony, induced a dreamlike state that helped him creatively. He not only produced a lot of copy, but what he did proved to be good and required very little revision.

Early, very early morning writing—in the case of another writer—produced a similar dream-like state comparable to that condition induced by the train. The darkness surrounding his spot-lighted typewriter, the utter quiet and sense of aloneness and his not being completely awake as yet contributed to the effect.

"Somehow," he said, "I had fewer inhibitions —working early in the morning. Maybe it takes being fully awake to be aware of all there is to be afraid of—imagined, and real."

When you work doesn't matter. Work, when you work most efficiently and with the greatest amount of pleasure. The important thing is that you write. And if you enjoy writing, you'll write more.

The spare-time writer must cultivate the knack of writing on order, his own order. Writing must appear on the page like a response to a stimulus.

Robert Penn Warren has this facility. He can, therefore, make full use of any quantity of free time.

As a friend of his said, with some amazement, "He simply goes to the typewriter, picks up where he left off, and pounds ahead."

Even in the matter of plotting, putting words down on paper is better, far better, than merely sitting and thinking. Write your thoughts. Call yourself names, in writing, if what you have thought is absurd. Tell yourself, in writing, what you still need to find to complete your story.

Write something like this, for example, "I need

a good juicy black moment. I need something to really jar the reader, make him feel that the hero will never get out of the jam he's in. Perhaps when the hero comes to meet the girl, she doesn't show up. He thinks that perhaps he misunderstood and he is supposed to meet her at his place. So when he goes there . . . Let's see, considering the girl's character, what might he find? Maybe he witnesses something that is not in her character at all. What could it be that he sees? Perhaps . . ."

Writing away in this manner, more ideas will come to you in five minutes than you can think of in an hour. This is a method that is especially valuable to you as a spare-time writer, for you're putting words down on paper and at no time do you feel that you've run hopelessly into the dead end of a plot.

To get started writing, use any trick or approach that will work for you. Sometimes, just sitting down with paper and pencil may seem less formidable than working at the typewriter. Then, by all means, use paper and pencil. And, when it suits your mood, switch back to the typewriter.

If yellow paper, which means a first draft, works better for you than white paper, which stands for finished copy, stick to yellow paper.

Whatever works for you—that is, a steady flow of copy coming out of your typewriter—is the right approach. Search it out, by trial and error. Use it. Don't apologize for it because it is different—even vastly different—from the working methods of others.

You may find that you need the discipline of a course in writing in order to get started and to gain the momentum that will keep you going on your own. From a writing-prolifically standpoint, study at home is better than a weekly trek to a classroom. How fast you go is then completely up to you. However, a correspondence course may simply not be for you. To be stimulated, your temperament may require direct, personal contact with a teacher—and the presence of other students who share your interests and your objectives. Many universities have journalism departments, offering adult courses, evening classes, summer programs. By making inquiries, you should find just what you want.

And once you get started writing, you—as a spare-time writer—must be especially responsive to the words that come to you out of nowhere, or the subconscious, as it has been glibly labeled. Put them down quickly, with only a slight, evaluative hesitancy. You will find that they are usually apt and can't be improved upon.

The times that you are writing especially well and fluently, you will invariably feel a certain excitement about what is going down on the paper before you, and it will carry you away from the bare outline or summary or idea from which you are working. You may find yourself expanding something in an entirely new and different direction—going on because of this feeling that you have that what you are doing is good.

The catalyst for this sort of performance is a pressure of sorts. The desire to spill your guts, or entertain, or instruct blended with the desire to get on with it. This pressure must not be burdensome; it must merely be a gentle goad.

The feeling that you will have, when excitement and pressure are in just the right proportions, will be of sailing along exhilaratedly.

Though there are relatively few things that will get you under way, the possible interruptions are without number. Then, too, there are quite a few things that will "just come up" to keep you from even getting started.

I've already mentioned the talkative man on your seat in the train. He takes many forms, none of them speechless.

Then there are the staple rationalizations, typified by, "So what if I don't work this time?" When you use this one, you are being humble. You imply, pleasurably, that keeping the spigot of your prose turned off for a time isn't going to make or break the world. There's no arguing that, either.

Another approach is to cover your not working with, "Oh, I'm just lazy that's all," and smile when you say it, implying that though you may be lazy, you are a good guy, who doesn't take himself too seriously and who has a terrific sense of humor.

Then there's that analogy of dubious validity. It skips along like this: A tennis player doesn't play tennis for awhile. You'd think that this lay-off would make him stale, wouldn't you? But it doesn't. When he resumes play, he's better than when he stopped. The answer, of course, is that he'd never really stopped, not in a complete sense. While he lay in the hammock, his right arm hanging limply over the gunwale, his subconcious worked furiously on his faulty backstroke. The conclusion to be drawn from all this is that it might be a nice, relaxing idea to get away from the typewriter for awhile.

And if you really want to keep from writing in your spare-time, don't worry; you'll get all kinds of help. In this connection, you'll find your wife to be just wonderful. She'll find things for you to do around the house, that after a hard day's work you could never have thought of all by yourself.

Then there's your wife, per se. She's home all day long, doing a few things around the house, but in the main living for the moment when she hears your very individual and beloved tread approach the door. So how are you going to eat dinner and go off and shut yourself up in another room with your typewriter? Even if she says, "I understand, dear. Just go ahead and play with your words. It's perfectly all right." Being the sensitive guy you are, however, you don't miss that single, perfect tear in its fall from eye to cheek curvature, as your wife bravely releases you for an evening of work.

Being a writer, by nature if not in fact, you're compassionate. You've got the whole world in your hands. So what you do is take your wife in your arms and kiss away that tear. "To hell with it," you tell yourself. "So I'll work two nights a week, instead of three."

Then there's social life, which, of course, also involves your wife—and your friends. You can't be a stick-in-the-mud, or a hermit, or anti-social, or a world all to yourself. You have to spend quite a bit of time at the typewriter, but you also definitely must get out and have a good time with people, real, live, nonfiction people.

Social life is versatile; it can interfere with your writing in all sorts of ways and it can also help it. The spare-time writer must gauge how much of it he wants, how much his time permits, how much is actually beneficial. Such calculation may seem cold, but calculation usually is—especially, if you want to get the right answer.

In this connection, one's own children pose quite a problem. As a parent, you feel duty-bound to spend some time with them. No matter what their age, you will be older than your children and your viewpoint will be different. You may love your kids, nonetheless. But there are those who have a low threshold of pain, and so the amount of time parents spend with children varies.

I am pleased to report that love has the edge on hate as a driving force for the spare-time writer. This includes love of oneself, of creditors, and of thy neighbor's wife. If you love your own kids, and your own wife, you will probably write more and better, too.

Another factor to be considered in the matter of writing prolifically in your spare time is the nature of your 9 to 5 job.

Many spare-time writers feel that if they could trade their particular job for an editorial job, they would be all set. In the main, this is a misconception.

First, I would like to point out the advantages of having an editorial job as your full-time job, while writing in your spare time. For one thing, you acquire an understanding of the whole editorial process—and this is invaluable. You see why manuscripts are accepted; why they're rejected; how they're edited. And by participating in the entire routine—issue after issue, or book after book—it becomes a part of you.

An editorial job may also give you the disdain of confidence. A writer told me that she hadn't thought of being a writer until she had been an editor for awhile.

"I worked on manuscripts written by name writers," she said. "And some of the stuff needed heavy editing. Well, I got the feeling that I could do as well as these big name boys did. And the thought of making their kind of money, let me tell you, was awfully appealing."

Still, going from your editorial desk to your spare-time writing desk has at least one pretty serious drawback. The work in both cases is too similar. You sit. You juggle words. But should your full time job consist of plumbing or delivering letters or driving a cab, you might more readily look forward to a stint at the typewriter. So, it can safely be said, that the greater the difference between your full-time and your spare-time job, the easier it is to switch from the one to the other.

The time has come to point out that some publishers forbid their editors to write in their spare time. Their editors may do anything else in their spare time, anything at all, from bowling to sex orgies, but they must not write. Back of this ordinance is the belief that if an editor gets too involved in writing, his heart won't be completely in his editing.

But editing, and allied jobs, tend to give an individual a special incentive and drive to write in his spare time. After awhile, editing may be viewed as menial. And working on someone else's writing, instead of one's own, may become irksome. So an editor may labor in his spare time, with the idea in the back of his mind that eventually he will give up editing altogether.

A veteran newspaperman told me. "It's wonderful being a newspaperman, for a short time. But if you stick with it too long, it'll ruin you as a writer. And I've seen it happen."

So, many newspapermen are driven to a more creative writing, which they must do in their spare time. And this is true of advertising copywriters and those who write for the movies.

Their choice is usually fiction. But nonfiction shouldn't be overlooked. Though it does present special problems; so nonfiction may not be for you. Whether it is or not, depends—in large measure—upon the amount of pleasure writing nonfiction can give you. The hedonistic yardstick must be applied to all writing—especially to spare-time writing—for if you don't derive fun from it, you're not going to continue at it for very long.

To enjoy doing nonfiction, you must enjoy research. This is the case because research is more than half the work. Actually, as much as seventy-five per cent of your time may be taken up with research. Aside from whether you enjoy it or not, research may be difficult to fit into a spare-time schedule if a considerable amount of interviewing is involved. To cite an extreme example, the definitive biography of Sinclair Lewis by Mark Schorer required that well over a thousand persons be interviewed.

The personal experience piece, obviously, doesn't require research. It's therefore ideal for a spare-time arrangement. But since such a piece has to be based on an uncommon experience like building a submarine in your back yard or reducing on five square meals a day, the number of such pieces that you can do is of necessity limited.

For some writers, doing both fiction and non-fiction is the answer. The writer then does whichever suits his purpose best at a particular time.

No matter what you write in your spare time, if you write prolifically and sell a respectable percentage of your copy, it is inevitable that you will begin to toy with the idea of quitting your job in order to write full time.

But you should interrupt this pleasant dream,

in which you are your own boss, writing when you want to and in whatever part of the world suits your fancy, to ask yourself a fairly important question.

"Can I," you should ask, "make enough money writing in my spare time to pay the rent and buy a little food once in awhile?"

You may reason, with what appears to be logic, that if you can make a certain amount of money writing ten hours a week, you should be able to turn out four times that much copy in a forty-hour week and make four times as much money. Two more questions that you certainly won't like to ask of yourself, should be asked: 1. Can I write four times as much as I'm writing in my spare time? 2. And if I am able to write four times as much, would I automatically make four times as much money?

I know one writer who turned with great elation and enthusiasm from spare-time to full-time writing. He'd figured every angle. He was sure he had it licked. Then, to his horror, he discovered that he had written more in his spare time than he did when he devoted all of his time to writing. He admitted that he missed the security of a weekly pay check. And because of this lack in his life, he found it impossible to write easily and quickly, expressing himself naturally. One thought always loomed like a dark, threatening cloud in the fore part of his head, "Will it sell?"

His first rejection, as a full-time writer, hurled him into a state of panic. What hurt him was not that his story had been rejected, but that a full week's work had been. And what if further submissions didn't sell the thing? That would mean that he had worked an entire week for nothing.

This was the spare-time writer who thought he had figured every angle—in the psychology and economics areas, too. Unfortunately, he had to give up his dream in a hurry and go back to spare-time writing.

The principal mistake this writer had made, when switching from spare-time to full-time writing was in doing speculative writing. If you turn full-time, free-lance writer, in order to survive you must reduce the speculative element of what you do to a minimum. Any hours or days that you work without a contract or an assignment, is time for which you may never receive remuneration. So if you're doing an article, send a query and get a go-ahead before doing the article. The query itself, you will find, is a considerable investment of time.

Some magazines will say that they would like to see the piece, as described in your query, but can't promise an acceptance or payment. Others offer conditional go-aheads: the payment of a few hundred dollars, even if they don't buy the piece. This is the kind of jungle growth through which you must find your way, circling daintily around the quicksand and sprinting when a fairly smooth piece of terrain shows up.

The question of how individual writers write

is often raised. There are those who want desperately to believe that good writers should be undernourished. They admire Stephen Crane for having died at the age of twenty-eight, felled by tuberculosis which had been enhanced by money-worries. And they insist that next to a writer's not being recognized in his lifetime, poverty just can't be beat for lending a writer a romantic air.

I'm therefore sorry to say that all writers, so it seems, write faster and better if they know they're going to be paid for their output. It's just one of those quirks of human nature that one can't do much about. Of course, if you're writing in your spare time, you can afford to write for the pure love of it, but this obviously can not be done if your writing must provide you with a livelihood. So payments for articles should be guaranteed. Contracts and initial payments should be obtained, in the case of books, for a few chapters and an outline. Forget the short story—for they have been stamped speculative—unless an editor should order one from you; but this sort of thing is rare.

And you might look into the matter of being subsidized by a publisher. This sort of arrangement didn't agree with Sherwood Anderson, but it has helped others get work done.

During the depression, when John O'Hara had no money, but a lot of debts, he also had 25,000 words of APPOINTMENT IN SAMARRA. He used those 25,000 words to induce a publisher to pay him fifty dollars a week for three months.

And during that three-month period, he finished the novel.

Nelson Algren had an even better arrangement. He asked a publisher for fifty dollars a week for a year so that he could write a novel for them. Because this publisher wanted Algren to write for them, he graciously consented to pay Algren sixty dollars a week for two years. The novel that Algren wrote for the considerate publisher was THE MAN WITH THE GOLDEN ARM.

There is one and only one moral to be deduced from all this: Don't quit your job too soon, but be happy writing prolifically in your spare time.

Chapter Five

INSIDE EDITORS, AGENTS AND PUBLISHERS

O NE of the important tenets of natural child-birth is this: the possibility of pain during labor is less likely if the expectant mother is not tense with fear. And the best way of giving her confidence and a feeling of security is through knowledge—a knowledge of all that transpires during childbirth—a familiarity with the maternity ward and with its techniques.

Now to make an analogy. In the land of the hackneyed, an author's story or book is likened to a baby, and getting them out of his system to childbirth. And if his special kind of child-birth is to be natural, in order that he have the assurance needed in the delivery room, he should not only know as much as possible about his craft, but about publishing—about editors, agents, publishers.

Writers who don't know editors at first hand must of necessity imagine what they're like. The result is a composite, blending fantasy and fact. The editor is a glamorous individual on the eighty-third floor, seated behind a vast desk that faces a glass wall that gives him a panoramic view of the western hemisphere; he is a sage, a dictator (a sadistic sonofabitch), libertine, saint (especially when he buys), frustrated writer (especially when he makes changes); he, in short, is anything a particular writer wants him to be.

There is, of course, the more accurate picture: a mortal—and therefore somewhat harried individual—stooped with the burden of his reading, the possessor of a tic or two (sometimes, this is no more than an anxious peering over the left shoulder at the deadlines that hound him), husband, father (wife, mother), employee, week-end and evening writer, mortgagee, and loyal friend. (A description of him somehow tends to resemble the notices which lodges run about their recently deceased brothers.)

The editor—all notions to the contrary—is more often governed by circumstance than by whim. There are usually reasons, decidedly rational reasons for the editorial changes he makes. By coincidence, all the stories that he has for an issue may have the same word in their titles. And this is simply because when a script is done for a mystery magazine, for example, the word murder is as natural a word to use in a title as is love in a slick paper title or Whither in a title for the "quality" magazines. So titles must be changed.

A writer once said to me, "I can understand all the changes you made in my script, but will you please tell me why you changed the name of the hero from Sam to Joe?" I told him. There was another Sam in the issue.

Cutting lines out of a story may have no more complex or vicious motivation. Say an illustration is to be fifty-five lines in size and the artist erroneously does a sixty-five line illustration, some cutting, therefore, has to be done. Since cutting ten lines out of an illustration would be something of a problem, ten lines are cut out of the text. Or cutting might be found necessary, for no other reason than that room must be made for an ad.

Then there are simple changes that might puzzle, and sometimes infuriate, the writer, when he compares his story as he wrote it with the published story. Makeup and the aesthetic rule that a partial line—termed a widow in the trade—must be filled is the cause of many simple changes. If "leaving his colleague to pay the check" doesn't fill the top of a column, changing "to pay the check" to "to take care of the check" might be made merely to fill the line.

There are also, of course, the more significant editorial changes that are made to clarify or to strengthen or to make a good story even better —or a faulty story, an acceptable one.

But the really professional writer doesn't go into a decline when his work is "tampered" with in this way. Primarily, sales, and all that they imply, are what interest him. And so a rejection bothers him more than a not-too-significant editorial change. He's out to please the editor and, at the same time, himself, and he always wants to leave the best possible impression.

There are writers, however—usually beginning ones—who go out of their way to alienate editors; they sometimes manage this before a manuscript of theirs is read.

A case in point is the letter-to-the-editor that accompanies the story. It is better—from the editor's standpoint—if this communication be brief and a clear statement. Always bear in mind that the editor may not only be human and subject to impressions—pro or con—regarding a writer's work, but he may also even be intelligent and perceptive.

In this brief and straight-to-the-point letter, don't timidly fail to tell about the sales you've made to the *Atlantic Monthly* or the new novel you sold to Knopf. (If the novel was published fifty or more years ago, it might be a good idea not to mention it.) Dear Unsure Writer, remember that there are editors who also have their uncertainties. Names may therefore impress them and be the needed weight on the balance. So relax and let the name drop.

And in this brief letter, it is not a good idea, if you haven't sold, to go to great lengths in proclaiming that fact. We have received letters which state that the manuscript accompanying it is a first effort, that it is therefore of dubious merit, and that the editor shouldn't bother to return it, after having read some of it, but to toss it in the round file.

Almost as bad is the letter that mentions tiny sales; that such sales do not impress is something of an understatement.

And almost as bad is the letter that is merely a query, which at great, involved length asks if the editor would like to see an extremely short story that he has written. He summarizes the story, informs the editor that it would make a wonderful movie, and points out who should be cast in the various roles and that he would be the best person to do the screenplay. He also amiably promises to lengthen the story if it is too short and shorten it if it is too long, explains that though this is his first try at fiction he has sold a filler to the Witchita Poultryman—a small, but very popular, periodical in his neck of the woods. He, incidentally raises chickens—white leghorns. Then there's a postscript that states that the editor should forget the whole thing if he's not prepared to give the writer movie rights, for he's sure it ought to make a good movie and that's why he has to have movie rights, and, come to think of it, he wants it stipulated in the contract that he must be the one to do the screenplay.

But this is only one of the ways used by beginning writers to make the editor take a long, weary breath and exhale it slowly. And these devices invariably stem from uncertainty. One device is the use of fancy pseudonyms. But why if a man's name is Melvyn Schmitz, does he anglicize his given name to something like Keith, or fabricate a name like Sann in order to burden a script with the byline Sann Schmitz? Or why should Alice Monroe believe that changing Alice to Alyce is going to make the difference between success or failure?

And an editor may understandably prejudge a manuscript when the word-count, in the upper right-hand corner of the title page, is down as "approximately 8,402 words," or when the first sheet is pristine white and fresh, but the rest of the script is a scorched yellow, folded and so worn at the folds that should it be held to the light, the holes across the page are like tiny beads on a string, or if the script is single-spaced, or written with a ball-point, or accompanied by blurb and homemade illustrations.

These are the sort of things that make it possible for an editor to start rejecting a manuscript before he's read it.

And a writer's lack of confidence may show in a variety of ways; this is true of both professional and amateur. There's the disease of trying too hard—endemic, and easily spotted. (One of the objectives of rewriting and polishing is to make a script appear to have been done without effort.)

Or treatment and plot may be familiar, simply because the writer is afraid to express himself and give individuality to his work. In self defense, he may bleat that he is only trying to give the editor what he wants and that if he doesn't do this what chance does he have of selling. It is true that an editor may say that a particular script is "not his sort of thing," and that the writer should slant more closely to his market. Even so, this does not mean that an editor does not want a writer's best work or that certain restrictions or ground rules should make excellence impossible. Though there's the limitation when writing a sonnet that it be held to fourteen lines and that its rhymes be arranged according to certain very definite schemes, this hasn't kept some poets from writing good sonnets.

The manuscript that an editor welcomes above all others is the one which doesn't need any editing. This is so primarily because such a script can virtually be put in the works just as it is and is a help in the meeting of deadlines. Generally, if a script requires little if any editing, it is also an indication that the script is, basically, a good one.

Of course, not all good writers are painstaking writers. But many are. Everything about their manuscripts is just right. Nothing needs to be cut or added. Spelling and syntax are invariably right. Should a geographical spot be mentioned, the editor can be sure the spelling has been checked, the location verified. Understandably, when a manuscript has this stamp of care, the editor has more confidence in the writer.

And the editor automatically feels confidence in a writer who he feels has confidence in himself. And he infers this confidence on the part of the writer in various ways. For one thing, the story's treatment may be fresh and appealing, and immediately catch the editor's interest. And the editor may feel as he reads that the writer has heard the words as his characters have spoken them and checked them with his ear for accuracy, and that he has seen the action as on a dim, dark screen, and here, too, on the part of the writer there has been an instantaneous hefting for genuineness, for credibility. The writer has obviously written—without inhibition or tension— what he has heard, and has described what he has seen.

And because the writer has been sure of himself, he is able to be original in his plotting. Even when he uses a familiar plot, he may approach it so differently that the reader is not aware that here once again is, say a boy-meets-girl epic or a domineering mother drama. I, for example, was inundated by stories of either a husband killing a wife, or a wife killing a husband, or of their simultaneous attempts to kill each other. When they start off as baldly as this one, for example, I despaired. "John decided to kill Emma that morning. It was at the breakfast table. It was the third morning in a row that she had burned the toast . . ." Then there's the professional-killer-paid-to-do-a-particular-job story. It, too, can start off so obviously that you know immediately not only its genre, but its inevitable conclusion. But when you get a story of this kind which, right off, tells you that the professional killer has been hired to kill someone and that that someone is himself you know immediately that you have a story worthy of serious consideration. Incidentally, this story's development and resolution lived up to the provocative quality of its initial situation. I bought the story.

All this may cause you to conclude that the writer should be solely concerned with pleasing the editor. As I've already said, the confident, prolific writer is more likely to be intent on pleasing himself. What he puts into his story is what he—almost as an objective outsider—wants to see there. The assumption on his part is that this will also be what the editor likes and that the editor, in turn, will feel that his readers will also be entertained by what both he and the writer like.

And because the editor is human—impressionable, prejudiced, and subject to sedentary aches and pains—he is not only able to put himself in the writer's place, but does. Should he also happen to be a writer, his empathy will be all the more thorough and profound.

When an editor, for example, isn't able to read a manuscript promptly, he knows what the writer off in Kenosha or San Francisco is thinking. He knows he is thinking, "I should have had a report by this time. They must really be considering my script seriously. Should I write and ask about it? But maybe if I do, they'll send it right back. Maybe I ought to wait another week. Yeah . . . another week . . . But it's certainly been a long time. God Almighty, it must have been read by this time. Then again, could be they're just getting some other readings on it. Or . . . could it be that it's lost? I wonder if I ought to write and ask them if they got it. But they must have. After all, when is something lost in the mail? Not very often. Maybe the thing's just under a pile of manuscripts and nobody's even looked at it. But, usually, by now, I'd have had a report . . ."

And because an editor knows, and compassionate ones care, the writer is usually assured kindly consideration. (Even printed rejection slips are composed with general solicitude, and with the archtype of thin-skinned writers in mind.)

For instance, every editor tries to salvage any script that merits saving. This is not pure altruism; it is not even altruism; it is merely a way of shoring up a shaky inventory. But suggested revisions may not only keep a script that may have holes in it from going under, but may improve it, and conceivably, teach the writer something.

Here are some random excerpts from correspondence I have had with writers, by way of illustration:

"I like . . . with certain reservations. I assume that your heroine is a psycho, and I feel that the weirdness of her make-up could be pointed up just a bit throughout the script. To the had-I-but known quality, should be added an overtone of eeriness. There is a suggestion of eeriness now, but I don't think it's strong enough. I also feel that the difficulty between her and her husband should be made a little clearer, and I gather that what is wrong in their relationship is that she is off her rocker.

"One other thing, she kills the man at the end of the story far too easily. I think that this should be gone into in some detail, to make it more convincing, and that you should aim at shock rather than gruesomeness. Of course, you will have to handle this carefully so that it does not destroy the effect of that final punch line . . ."

And here's another example of my attempt to save a script: "I like . . . by . . ., but I feel that it is overlong, and therefore drags a bit. I think that it can stand cutting throughout. If . . . agrees with me, and cuts the script, I'd certainly like to see it again."

The script was cut, I saw it again, and we bought it.

Of course all letters cannot be letters of acceptance, or even ones holding out the promise of a sale. This typifies the sad ones: ". . . has a compelling story situation. And its concluding bit of business is also good. What bothers me is all that goes between the beginning and the end; it lacks clarity and a dramatic build." (If this had gone to the writer rather than to his agent,

I probably wouldn't have written, "What bothers me is all that goes between the beginning and the end.") And here are a few more rejections that were sent to agents: "My report on . . .'s stories, I'm very sorry to say, must repeat what I've said before: the writing is individual and good, but their plots are too slight for us. As you know, we have to think of a mass audience, and for a mass audience the story or plot's the thing. I hope . . . doesn't give up as far as our magazine is concerned, for he writes exceptionally well, and quality writing is one of our requirements . . ." And here's another, ". . . must go back to you. This story's situation is a very familiar one: criminals moving in on an innocent family and taking over. Do you have anything else by . . . that I might see? If not would she do something expressly for us?"

Then there is the letter that cannot possibly be improved upon: "I like . . . very much. It's a beautifully written and plotted job. I can offer you a total price of . . . for it, and I'm enclosing a purchase order."

The correspondence relationship of editor and writer also includes letters from the writer to the editor. This one came in answer to a suggested revision: "We both understand that the script was originally meant to have so-called slickness. If I'd been doing it for you, I would have tackled it very differently. So I tried to think back and the result is that I have started it in a different place and I have cut, almost exclusively, the woman's mag. stuff. All the beginning is gone—all the pensive backward thoughts, brassieres, interior decor, dishwashing and bathing. And boy doesn't meet girl and discuss borrowing sugar. Hope you approve.

"A point though: One can cut atmosphere, style, plot, sheer redundancies, and lots of other things —but not characterization. Once written, characters are set in their molds and to cut them away is to leave just nothingness. Jerry is woman's-mag. noble; Karen is woman's-mag. sweet. I've toned 'em down, but I can't excise and have anything left, even a story . . ."

And these two excerpts illustrate the personal relationship that frequently develops between an editor and a writer, relationships in which painful problems are poured out and triumphs (what else would you call the sale of a first novel?) are shared. The first excerpt is from a writer who'd gone on from magazine short story writing to jobs in Hollywood studios: "Hello, from the land of pythons, nymphos and thick malted milks. I'm getting to feel like a pea in a shell game, the way I keep turning up under these various letterheads." (His jobs had been in one studio after another.) "But Hollywood is a jungle and if one is to survive one must go through the experience of being ground into all its meat grinders and still come to the surface with tongue and integrity in cheek . . . Each day I'm confronted by the awful, enervating truth of the place—a writer can exist without ever seeing a project he's given sweat and sleepless nights to, reach actual fruition. Having recently completed 8½ frightful months with . . . . I feel I can speak as the mother superior of all hacks. . . . . is like no animal alive—he eats people like you and me and doesn't even have the decency to wipe his chin between belches. Someday when the wounds have healed we'll sit over a New York lunch and I will tell you of the cannibals I have known. My project at this studio is still vague and in the outline stage, but at least the people are articulate in their vagueness. Anyway, hopes are high and the atmosphere is encouraging . . ."

Far more cheerful is this news from another writer: "I'm still in a daze; the typewriter keys before me are blurry. . . . just called me and told me that . . . have taken my Civil War novel. I wanted you to know the incredibly good news right away . . ."

No matter what your experience with editors has been, the all important thing is that when you send a script out, be confident it's all right, that it's the best you can make it, that it will sell—if not the first time out, eventually, inevitably. And though you should listen to the comments of those who read it—agent, editors, friends, wife—don't be moved from the basic evaluation you have made of your work. (This happens frequently. You may feel that there is something wrong in a script, but stubbornly ignore your feeling; then when the editor points out the flaw, you admit—perhaps, only to yourself—that you knew the flaw all the time and are puzzled why you would not consciously recognize it and work to remove it.)

If you send out a script that you have doubts about, which you feel isn't up to your standard, it, very well, may not be up to your standard. Such a script may cause the person to whom it is sent to begin to have doubts about your ability. He will then—whether he be agent or editor— view your subsequent work with a biased eye and may, very likely, misjudge it. This is bad, but even worse is the possibility that he may inoculate you with his doubts.

No matter how strict you are with yourself and how objectively you view your work, rejections will come. But you mustn't let anything —even rejections—touch or lay a heavy hand on your confidence. This means you should never put all your hopes in one job, no matter how well it's been done. You may believe in a particular script and be fond of it, but you should never feel that if it doesn't sell all is lost. This feeling is usually the result of a writer's presentiment that a particular piece of writing will not only be published, but will gather in the subsidiary monies —book club, movies, stage play—and, incidentally, be a best seller. Naturally, when the thing is not even accepted by a publisher, it is quite an emotional blow and the loss of all those in-the-bag subsidiary sales equals a financial debacle.

If you're to survive as a writer, you should obviously never permit your career to be founded

on one such script. You have to be able to take
rejections in your stride, you have to be resilient,
you have to remember that the sapling that
doesn't bend in the storm breaks. To sum this
up with yet another bromide: this is much easier
said than done.

One should also know enough to get out of an
unsatisfactory rut. Irving Stone did. At the beginning of his writing career, he was doggedly determined to be a playwright—and failed time and
again; then he tried another form: popular
fictionalized biography. His first subject was Vin-
cent van Gogh, and Stone brought this tragic artist to life in the highly successful LUST FOR
LIFE. (17 publishers turned the manuscript down,
however; it took three years to sell it.) At this
point, Stone said, "I realized two things: one, that
I had no talent for dramaturgy; and two, that I
liked writing in biographical materials." As a result of this liking, he produced—without
interruption—the life stories of Jack London,
Clarence Darrow, Jessie Fremont, Eugene V.
Debs, Rachel Jackson, Mrs. Abraham Lincoln,
Michelangelo . . . .

The moral is obvious: be versatile until you find
your niche, until you discover what you like to do.
If you feel stymied, plagued by non-production and
rejections, perhaps you're attempting to work in
an area that's not right for you. Maybe you should
try writing greeting cards, or juveniles, or poetry,
or TV scripts, or . . . . You'll not only be more prolific if you branch out into something different, but
will also be happier. This doesn't mean that there

won't be problems—and rejections. Versatility also entails taking chances; taking it on the chin. However, you must always remember that editors can be wrong—17 were in Irving Stone's case— and that you, *you*, can be right.

As further proof of all this, consider the following account. I turned to biography when my wife came across fascinating letters touching on the deteriorating Theodore Roosevelt-William Howard Taft friendship. Although I considered myself a novelist, I found this dramatic situation too intriguing to pass up. I therefore wrote a chapter and an outline of a proposed Roosevelt-Taft book, and they went to my agent and then to prospective publishers. (The names of publishers and editors, in what follows, have been withheld to protect well-meaning ones.)

The first rejection sounded an especially ominous note; it reminded me that I, a novelist, had strayed into biography. The editor wrote, ". . . the fact that he has not attempted anything of this nature before does raise a slight question in my mind . . . ."

With metronome regularity, the rejections continued to come, each one different, but all in effect the same.

Number two proclaimed: "I'm afraid that in a case like this I would need 70 or 80 pages of good solid text to convince me that we should sign him up."

(Agent's note, accompanying rejection: "I think we ought to try more places before you sit down to do 70 or 80 pages, which I think is asking too much." Oh, I agreed with her! She was on *my* side . . . !)

Then a rejection arrived that belonged in the small-comfort department: ". . . If you aren't able to sell this project on the basis of the chapter and outline we saw, and Manners proceeds to write more I would very much like to be given the chance to read any and all the material he produces. As I said before, I find his prose extremely professional, and if anyone can make the subject interesting and readable, I'm sure he can. Thanks again for letting me see it."

Then, as though for a touch of variety: ". . . our sales people just did not see any solid sales potential—at least for (publisher's name)—in the subject."

Of course, I had to wait between rejects, and I found the anguish to be precisely the same when waiting for word on a biography as it had been for word on a novel.

Hopes are raised in exactly the same way in both genres, when there's no word from a publisher for an inordinately long time. In this particular instance—when word finally came—I learned: "I'm sorry to have kept TR AND WILL by William Manners so long, but quite frankly it was difficult coming to a decision about it. The manuscript has some very interesting material and is another fine example of Mr. Manners' writing ability. I do not feel, however . . . ." (What joy was there in the knowledge that the publisher had writhed in the throes of decision making? So he might have said yes, but he did say no. As for my "writing ability," obviously it hadn't produced a fine enough example this time.)

With my next rejection, I arrived at the half-dozen mark. The most I could say for this rebuff was that it smacked of ad hominem, vindictiveness, and flippancy. "Manners does present his material vividly, but from the outline and sample chapter, I am not sufficiently persuaded of his political insight. Thanks for giving me a looksee." Looksee? *Looksee?*

Rejections were beginning to erode my innate affability. My wonderful agent who was on my side sensed this, for on the bottom of the next one she scrawled: "I *am* sorry. I am continuing. Onward and upward!" This rejection complained that what I had done was "lacking in intimacy," that the story had been "told from the outside rather than from within."

Then this one came: "Considering the voluminous biographies of Teddy Roosevelt and Taft that have already been written, I'm not at all sure that Manner's idea would support a full fledged book at this time . . . ."

Next, my agent received a letter from Harcourt, Brace & World that was filled with delights: "We are, at the moment, quite taken with the idea and with the sample chapter, and we'd like very much to explore the possibilities further with you and Mr. Manners . . . in the event of our signing the book . . . get together for lunch to talk things over . . . if December 2nd is at all possible for you and Mr. Manners, we'd be well pleased . . . ."

On December 16th, we met for lunch; on December 23rd, Harcourt, Brace & World purchased TR AND WILL; December 25th was an electrically charged Christmas; and January 1st seemed like a good, beginning-of-the-year time to start writing and writing and writing in an area completely new to me.

Such happy endings are a long time in coming. Sometimes you may know only defeat.

In this time of trial, you should feel perfectly free to hate an editor who has rejected a script of yours. You may view him as an incompetent, visualize him as a brute who has tossed your script into the maw of first readers. You may say his magazine is constantly running stuff that's not nearly as good as yours. And though you may be too busy turning out other stories to be overly bothered by a rejection, and though this is the better approach, hating editors is undeniably a considerable pleasure.

But hate and bitterness and despondency, and worse, are understandable. They may not solve anything, but they are still understandable. Walter Kerr has said, "For the playwright, a three-performance flop is a total flop from which nothing can be salvaged and nothing can be learned. Its demise is so abrupt, and its dismissal so absolute that the dramatist, writhing in embarrassment and sick to his soul, can only conclude that his work was utterly worthless."

So one shouldn't be glib about rejections.

I know an editor who has this reminder over his desk: "A writer is an anemone, and an anemone is a tender plant." It's true, too, more often than not. A writer told me that over a quarter of a century ago, an English teacher, whose name he no longer remembers, commanded him in the margin of a theme to "think before you write." What hurt, the writer said, embittered even in retrospect, was that he had done a considerable amount of thinking before writing the theme. He also remembered another marginal comment: "a plethora of words." Not only hasn't he forgotten this temporally remote criticism, but he remembers that at first he took it to be a compliment until he looked up plethora in the dictionary.

Granted that writers are a particularly sensitive lot and granted that some rejections are inevitable and granted that rebuffs are hard to take, the best advice is that when the rejection-hurt comes, you're so busy with projects that you don't care —as much. The prolific writer takes criticism and outright rejection far better than the meager producer. And for much the same reason that the mother of many children may be in less of a dither than the mother of an only child.

To recapitulate, never permit your career to be founded on a single script—even one that sells, but doesn't prove nearly as successful as you were absolutely certain it would. Keep working, keep turning out copy—of all sorts. If you're a real writer, you have to write no matter what happens to your product. And, if you have something to offer, eventually its merit will be recognized. If you don't hit fame and the jackpot with one script, you will with another. At least that should be the essence of your confident attitude.

Agents, like rejections, may affect a writer's output and mental health. The beginning writer feels that all he needs is an agent in order to sell; many established writers believe that all they need do is get rid of their agent, and if they get another one—a good one, this time—all their problems would be solved.

Writers confide in me, and thereby, I assume, frequently experience a certain degree of therapeutic release. And I find that the agent is very often the butt of their aggressive feelings.

Here numerically, but not in order of significance or vehemence, are some of the complaints I have heard:

1. "I never know where my stuff's been sent. I know if I'd ask, he'd tell me. But he always seems so busy, I just don't like to ask."

2. "Face it, they got these best-selling authors and, naturally, they spend the time on them. The only reason they bother with me at all is on the off chance I might some day turn out to be a best-selling author. I'm not blaming them; that's just the way it is."

3. "So they mail my stuff out. Big deal."

4. "Anybody knows that you should shoot a script to the top markets first, and then work your way down to the little markets. He sent it right off to . . . and sold it. That's all very well

and good, but I believe it would have sold to *Playboy*, if it had been sent there. What's more, I suggested that he send the thing to *Playboy*."

5: "This agent of mine'll send a manuscript out to a couple of markets, and if it doesn't sell, he doesn't want to be bothered with it anymore. He doesn't want to gamble with the cost of sending it out."

6. "All they think about is their ten per cent."

7. "Ahhh, this outfit's got so many clients, they don't have time for any of them. I need an agent in order to get in touch with my agent."

8. "She's very nice. Maybe I say that because she praises everything I do. She's sure so and so will like it. It's a great improvement, she says. I'm making strides, she says. But does she sell any of this stuff that she raves about? Not up to now, she hasn't."

9. "By the time I get a report whether they're taking it on or not, I could have sent the thing out to a dozen places."

10. "I just don't agree with their judgment. Especially, when they think something that I've done is lousy, and it's really terrific. They think it's so lousy they don't even want to send it out."

The lament goes on and on . . .

But the agent does perform certain services. He relieves the writer, for one thing, of all the detail of marketing a script. This means a saving in time. Sending a script on its way, keeping track of where it goes and when, pondering over the problem of where it should go next, trying to determine the particular person in an editorial office to whom it should be sent—all these chores take time and if done by a writer, to some extent interfere with his writing.

There is also this advantage, when an agent is handling your work: you don't see the actual, physical manuscript that is rejected and returned. You may—or you may not, according to one of the enumerated complaints—hear from your agent that a script has been turned down. This, somehow, doesn't involve as many senses and emotions as going to the mail-box and seeing the 9x12 Manila envelope. And among the feelings experienced, there is very often the "maybe-I'm-no-good" feeling. You may also know that you should send the returned script out again, posthaste, either for the sake of efficiency or to prove to yourself that you have not been vanquished. But knowing all this you may still find yourself holding onto the script, for days or longer, wondering if you should send it out and to whom.

There is probably no perfect solution. But, unquestionably, if an agent by the very nature of his profession is going to interfere with your writing—both as to its volume and quality—by keeping you in a constant turmoil of doubts and misgivings, you will obviously be better off not having an agent. And for those who feel that an agent is not doing enough, it may be good idea to try supplementing the agent's work, by establishing personal contacts with editors. I know that many writers who have agents work directly with me, and I've found it to be a mutually beneficial arrangement.

A writer may also have a book publisher on his hands and the special psychological problems peculiar to book publication on his mind.

The best all-inclusive advice is to forget your just-published book and get on with the next one.

If it's a first book that's just been published, you may loiter in a book store around a one-copy display of the thing. You may permit yourself to feel famous. You may go from book store to book store and try to will browsers to go as in a trance to your book, to pick it up, to open it—even to buy it. (The cold, unfeeling laws of probability are, of course, against you.) You may be disturbed by the number of titles and by the multitude of books in a book store, while feeling pride that your book is a star in this galaxy of paper and print; you may tell the proprietor that you are the author of one, literally one, of the books that he is selling—actually, trying to sell, in a completely passive sense that is; you may bother the proprietor by frequent visits to his store, and—if it is consistent with your personality—annoy him with questions, belligerently spoken, concerning his failure to sell your book; and with such acts as bodily taking your book from its position inside the store and placing it precisely in the center of his window display, toppling other books, cataclysmically, in the process.

You may do all these things—and probably

will—upon the publication of your first book. You will also read the reviews. You will also subscribe to a clipping service, in order to know what a critic in Lubbock, Texas, has to say about your book. You should, if possible, be objective; so that even when a review is favorable, if it's stupid, you should say it's stupid. (Favorable reviews, like unfavorable ones, can be done without an understanding or a reading of the book reviewed.)

But even worse than bad intelligent reviews is the day upon which a book is published. What is breathlessly expected by the author is breathlessly vague but certainly, in expectation, the author walks in a not-completely-here champagne glow. But publication day starts like all other days with your getting up and looking at your tongue in the bathroom mirror, the newspaper headlines concern some violence somewhere, but there in glaring agate type in the column "Books Published Today," is the title of your book and your byline. After this promising beginning, the day, somehow, seems quieter than usual. By three o'clock in the afternoon you've decided that nothing of great moment is going to happen. The stillness grows more oppressive. And then when it's time to turn in for the night, and you realize that the day is irrevocably over, anything may set in, from the blues to thought of taking a life that may very well be your own.

The next morning, however, God's in his heaven, things look better. As you lie in bed, you recall that Virginia Kirkus made the prepublication prediction that your book was due to be on the best seller list. You are also reminded by a kindly inner voice that many smash literary successes have been slow starters. "My book is a slow starter," you think with sudden happiness. Sure enough, during the next few days, things start to happen—verbally. There's talk of a movie offer and talk of your going out to Hollywood because an interested producer wants to talk to you, talk to you about something relevant to your book, presumably. And there's a rumor that a top song writer wants to do a hit song based on the title of your book. Oh, yes, and someone at the Book-of-the-Month Club—and someone is just not anyone there—likes your book and this means that they're seriously considering it as a selection. (They also, it so happens, give serious consideration to what books they should review in the Book-of-the-Month Club News.)

Enjoy the anticipation of all these possible successes, be pleased and sanguine—there's no harm in that—but maintain a Missourian cynicism. As my mother used to say, "the girl shouldn't rejoice until the wedding ring is on the finger."

This attitude is important because should every glittering prospect collapse, then the blow is not as hard and won't affect your work as much. It might be a good idea to tell yourself before the final results are in that even if fame and fortune come your way, the core of your life will remain essentially the same: you'll continue to write so many hours a day and be absorbed by your work. You won't clamber out of the rut of your various personal habits. The one change that you would prize is the opportunity for certain new experiences (for the sake of your writing) that without these successes, you could not otherwise have.

And if your book doesn't go over in a big way, don't blame the publishers. (Though at the time this may be the more satisfying alternative. The other alternative, of course, is blaming yourself.) You may say that if they had publicized your book and advertised it, all would have been different. (Their indisputable answer: the advertising budget is determined arithmetically by dividing the total retail price of the print order and by multiplying.) You will blame them for having only one harried hell-of-a-nice guy to take care of the publicity for all authors and their books. (He will pay for all lunches and martinis and try to get you to drink as many of these as possible, because he knows the nature of your immediate future and is a hell-of-a-nice-guy.) You will regard as ridiculous the publisher's contention that if a book doesn't do well there's no point in advertising it, that reviews—good ones, naturally—are the best advertising in the world and if a book, therefore, doesn't get off the ground following the reviews, no amount of advertising will help it; as for publicity, there's no better publicity than word-of-mouth publicity. You will be sure—and righteously indignant—that publishers champion word-of-mouth publicity because it doesn't cost a cent and because it gives them the oh-so-grand and lordly feeling that they have a vast publicity staff.

Book publishers, especially if you as a writer have the usual paranoiac tendencies, will give you the feeling that your book is only one among many. When your book appears, you see, they are already hard at work on and excited about other books. (This treachery and unfaithfulness will be painfully hard to believe.) And your book, in a very real sense, is in desperate competition with the other books on the list and with books on the succeeding list. (Lists, incidentally, are euphemistically named after the four beautiful seasons of the year.) If one of these other books competing with yours sells to the movies or is picked by a book club, or happens to be written by a Salinger or a John O'Hara, then things are really tough for your book. You may begin to feel like Job and lament Biblically that the interest of the publisher is as intense as passion, but doth indeed wither like the grass. Or, if you are another sort, you may simply stick to profanity.

Knowing all these disturbing things, one must not be disturbed. Nor should one assume that there is a best book publisher or even a better book publisher; there are just book publishers. All publishers have the same fiscal problems and therefore, in the eyes of writers, the same weaknesses. It, therefore, doesn't make sense and is most enervating to search for *the* publisher.

If you feel that you have been manhandled by a publisher, allow one day for sulking on this score. Circumstances, on occasion, may even warrant a certain amount of self-pity. This takes time and energy and is habit forming—so it should be watched and carefully kept within bounds.

In short, and to recapitulate, if you're going to be a prolific writer—and therefore a reasonably happy one—don't let editor, agent, publisher, weather, inflation, PTA or yourself—especially, yourself—interfere with your work.

Chapter Six

WHERE TO GET HELP...
EMOTIONAL AND FINANCIAL

I F you're going to be a prolific writer, there is nothing wrong in being helped, emotionally, financially, or by simple advice or suggestion. Of course, some writers will not permit any of their work to be touched by an editor, regarding it all —imperfections included—as perfect. To these writers, the idea of help—which implies a lack on their part—is repugnant.

If this describes you, and you are pleasantly unhappy and writing voluminously and well, by all means don't change. This chapter is for those who know moments of loneliness, who have already made a loan on their life insurance and so they can't get any more money from that source, who think other writers are greater than they are, who require companionship and love, who need help and advice, who would still like to sell a script that has already made thirty-two round trips.

It's a good idea when doing a piece of writing, to know there is a specific market for it—and something about that market's requirements. Be assured that there is a seemingly endless number of markets. Take a look at the *Directory of Newspapers and Periodicals*, published by N. W. Ayer and Sons. It is 1,581 pages long, and all these pages are filled with small print. It includes everything that is being published from the *Advent Review and Sabbath Herald* to the *Wyoming Rural Electric News*.

All the major book publishing houses publish fiction of all types and non-fiction of all types. And if you are still in need of a market, don't overlook the paperback publishers, for many do originals—both fiction and nonfiction.

The market tips in the various writer's magazines are helpful; they tell what the magazine and book publishers are after, their word lengths, taboos, rates of payment, length of time it takes them to report, etc. However, market tips fluctuate like the weather. The editors who are listed in them fade away or take a desk elsewhere. (One I know of, ran off and joined a circus.)

The principal periodicals publishing market tips are:

> *The Writer*
> *The Writer's Digest*

Market lists, revised annually are to be found in:

> *The Writer's Year Book*
> *Writer's Market*
> *Literary Market Place*

The output of many writers has been reduced appreciably by a bromide that goes on and on and will not die. It states that the writer should write what he knows about. The implication is that his writing be circumscribed by his experience and that his experience does not include what he reads, learns, and discovers on extended flights of fancy. But Stephen Crane who hadn't been a soldier in the Civil War (he wasn't born until 1871, for one thing) wrote of soldiers under fire in that war, and did it so remarkably well that it made him famous. And a contemporary author, after assiduous research in the 42nd Street Library in New York City, came up with a novel concerning the life of an Eskimo family in its remote and frozen habitat.

Therefore, make use of whatever library facilities are available to you. Their indexes and guides will help you find the material you need. And so will their librarians—if you stoutly march up to them and ask for assistance. They frequently help to such an extent, the authors thank them by name at the beginning of the books they help make possible.

To get basic information concerning any book, in or out of print, use the *Cumulative Book Index*. (Librarians lovingly refer to it as CBI.) CBI is usually kept in a back room, but may be consulted upon request.

To locate magazine articles on a particular subject, use the *Reader's Guide to Periodical Literature*.

To find any newspaper story that has appeared in the *New York Times*, make use of the *New York Times Index*. This index will give you the date the story has appeared and something of its nature, and you will then have to find a library that has the *Times*—the very old papers are on microfilm—in order to read the story.

To uncover information on any subject, the *Guide to Reference Books* lists books for you in which you may find what you want.

To find out how a book was reviewed—and therefore something about it—consult the *Book Review Digest*. Excerpts from principal reviews are given.

This is only the merest of indications of what a library has to offer a writer.

And don't overlook universities. In getting started, some individuals require the assistance of a writing course. For information—for anything from editing to creative writing workshops—write to any of the following:

Columbia University, Writing Division, 116th & Broadway, New York, NY 10027

Hunter College, 695 Park Avenue, New York, NY 10021

Mystery Writers' of America, 105 East 19th Street, New York, NY 10003

New School for Social Research, 66 West 12th Street, New York, NY 10011

New York University, 2 University Place, New York, NY 10003

Northwestern University, 1845 Sheridan Rd., Evanston, IL 60201

Ohio University, Athens, Ohio 45701

Los Angeles City College, 855 N. Vermont Ave., Los Angeles, CA 90029

Another kind of help, that you should at least know about, is that provided by fellowships and grants. In order to do a certain piece of writing, your temperament may require a feeling of security—that is, the knowledge that the usual run of bills are going to be taken care of. (When Sherwood Anderson had an arrangement with his publisher for them to send a check at regular intervals, he found these checks interfered with rather than helped his literary output. So there you are.) You have to know what you as an individual require; and if it's the pressure of insecurity you need, you'll have to admit that this is the best of all possible worlds for that sort of thing. And should the Nobel Prize for Literature ever be offered to you, $130,000, you may quite blithely turn it down.

If you are eligible for any of the following, and they interest you, write for further information and an application.

Carnegie Fund for Authors
330 Sunrise Highway
Rockville Centre, N.Y. 11570

To an author who has had at least one book published, and is in acute financial need resulting from illness or injury to self, spouse, or dependent child, or some other misfortune. Amount of grant dependent on need.

Guggenheim Fellowships
John Simon Guggenheim Memorial Foundation
90 Park Avenue
New York, New York 10016

Opportunities to further research and artistic creation for scholars and artists of high ability. Grants are variable in amount. Each grant is adjusted to needs and other resources of the applicant.

Centro Mexicano de Escritores Fellowship
Centro Mexicano de Escritores
San Francisco 12,
Mexico 12, D.F.
   This fellowship is for Latin-American writers.
   $1,600 to $2,400.

Boston, Mass. 02107
   Fellowships given each year for projects in fiction or nonfiction by promising writers who need financial assistance to complete their work. $7,500. Of this amount, $5,000 is an advance against royalties and $2,500 is an outright grant.

Mary Roberts Rinehart Foundation Award
Mary Roberts Rinehart Foundation
516 Fifth Avenue
New York, N.Y. 10036

   To give aid and assistance to writers of creative ability who lack financial means to complete their work. Grants-in-aid of approximately $1,000 each.

Harper-Saxton Memorial Trust
Harper & Row, Publishers
10 East 53rd Street
New York, N.Y. 10022

   To creative writers who need financial assistance to complete projected books. Must submit minimum of 10,000 words and summary. $7,500—of which $5,000 is an advance against royalties and $2,500 is an outright grant.

National Institute & American Academy Grants
National Institute of Arts & Letters
633 West 155th Street
New York 32, N.Y.
Awarded to non-members to further creative work. Seven grants of $2,500 each.

Should you also require solitude—and at the same time the companionship of other writers—consider these:

Edward MacDowell Association, Inc.
1083 Fifth Avenue
New York, N.Y. 10028
Composers, artists, and writers of proved ability are invited by the Association to live at the Colony in Peterborough, N.H., for one to three months in the summer or winter. A chance is offered to concentrate on creative work.

Yaddo
c/o Executive Director
Saratoga Springs, N.Y. 12866
Expense-free haven for artists in Saratoga Springs; open to artists who have reached a high level of professional achievement in fields of writing, painting, musical composition.

Each summer across the country—east, west, mid-west—Writers' Conferences are held. They are from a few days to a few weeks in duration. A change of scene and intellectual stimulation may help you write more and better.

One Writers' Conference expresses in a general way the objectives of all Writers' Conferences. It was founded "on the premise that professional training in creative writing should be supplied by a recognized educational institution through the leadership of experienced writers. The policy of presenting as workshop leaders writers of outstanding reputation has attracted many students who now have impressive records of publication. The leaders have never presumed that writing could be taught, but students with talent and the desire to learn have benefited immeasurably from their professional criticism and direction. The atmosphere of the Writers' Conference is an informal and friendly one. Students and staff meet outside the workshops, in the dining room, and during social and recreational activities. Students find the informal exchange of ideas with other writers— faculty and students—a most valuable and enjoyable experience." (Former workshop leaders included John Mason Brown, Robert Frost, Dorothy Parker, Katharine Anne Porter, Elmer Rice, Carl Sandburg, Robert Penn Warren, Jessamyn West, Thomas Wolfe, and Philip Wylie.)

For more information, write to the director of any of the following:

Florida Writers' Conference, University of Florida, Gainesville, FL 32601

University of Oklahoma, Norman, OK 73069

McKendree Writers' Conference, McKendree College, Lebanon, IL 62254

Okland University Writers' Conference, Okland University, Rochester, MI 48063

Chautauqua Writers' Workshop, Chautauqua Institution, Chautauqua, NY 14722

Cape Cod Writers' Conference, Box 111, W. Hyannisport, MA 02672

Omaha Writers' Conference, Creighton University, Omaha, NB 68131

Georgetown University Writers' Conference, Georgetown University, Washington, DC 20007

Philadelphia Writers' Conference, Box 834, Philadelphia, PA 19105

La Jolla Summer Writers' Conference, University of California, La Jolla, CA 92093

Wesleyan-Suffield, Writer-Reader Conference, Wesleyan University, Middletown, CT 06457

Cornell University, Creative Writing Workshop, Ithaca, NY 14853

Bread Loaf, Middlebury College, Middlebury, VT 05753

Indiana University Writers' Conference, Indiana University, Bloomington, IN 47401

One final device that may help you to be more productive: books by writers about their work, or interviews of writers concerning their work may give you ideas, or inspire you, or help you in licking a particular personal problem. And so here are:

THE WRITER OBSERVED by Harvey Breit; World Publishing Co., 1956.

Over a period of four years the author conducted a series of talks with authors, resulting sketches were published in the *New York Times* and give you all sorts of material about the authors involved, their appearance, taste, working habits, opinions, etc.

AUTHOR'S CHOICE, 40 STORIES by MacKinlay Kantor; Coward-McCann, 1944.

The book's subtitle: "With copious notes, explanations, digressions and elucidations, the author tells frankly why he selected these stories, why they were written, how much money he received for them, and of his thrilling adventures with wild editors in their native haunts."

HOW TO WRITE AND SELL MAGAZINE ARTICLES by Richard Gehman; Harper & Brothers, 1959.

Fourteen articles which appeared in top national magazines and comments on them, the writing problems that each illustrates. There are chapters on making an outline, research methods, the lead, cutting and revising, etc. There is also some autobiographical material.

WRITERS AND WRITING by Robert Van Gelder; Scribner's, 1946.

Containing sketches of more than 100 authors, giving writing routines, biographical notes, hobbies, etc. Included are Ernest Hemingway, Sinclair Lewis, Sigrid Undset, William Saroyan, J. P. Marquand, James Norman Hall, Christopher Morley and Carl Van Doren. Articles appeared originally in the *New York Times Book Review*.

WRITING FOR LOVE OR MONEY, edited by Norman Cousins; Longmans, 1949.

35 essays reprinted from the *Saturday Review of Literature* in which are described the methods which each writer has found to be basic in achieving a successful piece of writing.

WRITING—FROM IDEA TO PRINTED PAGE;
Case Histories of Stories and Articles Published
in the *Saturday Evening Post*, by Glenn Gundell;
Doubleday, 1949.

From the book's introduction, "The material in
this book is not designed to serve as a text-
book on how to write. It is merely a record of
how individual writers and an artist went about
creating an acceptable product . . ."

THE MYSTERY WRITER'S HANDBOOK,
edited by Herbert Brean, Harper & Brothers;
1956.

The contributors are professionals, members of
the Mystery Writers of America, who have
achieved renown in the world of mystery writing. They give you fresh and valuable information on the tools and strategies of the mystery-
writing trade, as well as on their own writing
habits—when they write—what their greatest
stumbling blocks are, and what are the best
trade tricks they have discovered. Though this
book is aimed primarily at the production of
the mystery story, the advice and information
it provides can be applied with equal effect to
other forms of fiction.

I WANTED TO WRITE by Kenneth Roberts;
Doubleday, 1949.

Anecdotal, factual and sprinkled with diary
entries, it traces Mr. Roberts' career from college

through newspaper and magazine work to the writing of historical novels.

WRITERS AT WORK; *The Paris Review* Interviews, edited and with an introduction by Malcolm Cowley; Compass Books Edition, issued in 1959 by Viking Press.

16 authors are interviewed: E. M. Forster, Francois Mauriac, Joyce Cary, Dorothy Parker, James Thurber, Thornton Wilder, William Faulkner, Georges Simenon, Frank O'Connor, Robert Penn Warren, Alberto Moravia, Nelson Algren, Angus Wilson, William Styron, Truman Capote, Francoise Sagan. The interviews are in question and answer form. Each one is preceded by a short biographical sketch. From Malcolm Cowley's excellent introduction: "The editors of *The Paris Review* have been generous with their time and space, and the result is a series that seems to me livelier and more revealing than others of its kind. Unlike most of the others it is concerned primarily with the craft of fiction. It tells us what fiction writers are as persons, where they get their material, how they work from day to day, and what they dream of writing . . ."

WRITERS AT WORK; *The Paris Review* Interviews, second series, introduced by Van Wyck Brooks. Viking Press, 1963.

This second volume speaks abundantly for itself. The list of interviewees runs alphabetically from Lawrence Durrell through Boris Pasternak, S.J. Perelman, and Katherine Anne Porter. George Plimpton's celebrated interview with Ernest Hemingway is included, and, in a departure from the predecessor volume, five major world poets are represented: T.S. Eliot, Robert Frost, Robert Lowell, Marianne Moore, and Ezra Pound. The student of writing will especially appreciate the various methods of work which these interviews reveal. Each interview is graphically illustrated by a reproduction of a page of the author's manuscript, and there is an original portrait of each author. Van Wyck Brook provides a stimulating introduction.

A WRITER'S DIARY by Virginia Woolf; Harcourt, 1954.

Virginia Woolf began to keep a regular diary in 1915, and continued to do so until a few days before her death in 1941. Her husband has extracted from the diaries those passages which refer directly to Virginia Woolf's own writing, to her constant and omnivorous reading, and to scenes and people in her life.

AUTHOR! AUTHOR! by P. G. Wodehouse; Simon & Schuster, 1962.

Letters by Wodehouse in which plotting, characterization, story construction—in fact, every aspect of writing is touched upon.

FURTHER CONFESSIONS OF A STORY WRITER by Paul Gallico; Doubleday, 1961.

Gallico presents twenty stories, old and new, and tells how he wrote and sold them. Along the way, there are many valuable asides on agents, editors and magazines.

PEN TO PAPER by Pamela Frankau; Doubleday, 1962.

The author of thirty books shares her writing experience with the professional and amateur writer. Memoirs coupled with sound advice for writers.

WRITER'S ROUNDTABLE. Presented by the Author's Guild. Edited by Helen Hull and Michael Drury. Harper, 1959.

Twenty-one professionals—writers, editors, agents —combine in this handbook to offer the new writer valuable advice based on their experience and skill.

HOW TO MAKE MONEY WRITING MAGAZINE ARTICLES by Society of Magazine Writers. Edited by Beatrice Schapper; Arco Publishing Co., 1974.

Magazine article writers often exclaim, "If only I *could* watch an experienced pro as he goes about his work!" This book grants their wish. In it, eight members of the Society of Magazine Writers tell all. Each of the eight explains the how and why of his research steps; each reveals his writing quirks and methods; each evaluates his editor's contribution; and each tells how he overcame obdurate hurdles to get his piece published. "By learning the basics so clearly discernible in each chapter of this book," Beatrice Schapper says, "new writers can become published writers in as little as twelve weeks— many of my students have done so."

THE WRITING OF ONE NOVEL by Irving Wallace; Simon and Schuster, 1968.

Portrait of a writer at work on one of his novels, THE PRIZE. The book shows how the basic idea of a novel about the Nobel Prize awards took form over sixteen years; tells of the false starts, the persistent detective work to hunt down facts for use in fiction, the many drafts, the elation, the despair, the *work* inseparable from the writer's life and craft. Here, too, is the behind-the-scenes drama of publishing.

THE WRITER'S CRAFT, edited by John Hersey; Knopf, 1974.

A collection of writings by writers about writing that gives us insights into what it means to live by and for this craft. Throughout the book run threads of the craft's vital themes: What makes the writer's craft worth following through all its work and pain? What are a writer's true rewards? How is literature made? What are the sources, in the life of the writer, of what we call art? And what gives great writings their power?

THE WRITER'S VOICE, Conversations with Contemporary Writers; conducted by John Graham and edited by George Garrett; William Morrow, 1973.

The authors interviewed discuss their own

work, the work of others, the creative process—
in general, the craft of writing. These
interviews—free-wheeling, inventive, frank—
form an important contribution to the small
body of literature in which artists explain what
they are doing and how they go about doing it.

THE WRITER'S WORLD, edited and with an
introduction by Elizabeth Janeway; McGraw-Hill,
1969.
The result of thirteen panel discussions at The
New School for Social Research on the subject of
"Writers and Writing." Here are opinions and
convictions on every form of writing. The con-
tributors include Alfred Kazin, Leo Rosten,
Richard Rovere, Barbara Tuchman, Walter
Lord, Howard Taubman, Joseph Heller, Dwight
Macdonald, Bel Kaufman, Walter Kerr, Susan
Sontag, Isaac Singer, Marianne Moore, Shirley
Hazzard, and John Cheever.

Chapter Seven

WRITING'S MANY REWARDS

THE prolific writer is integrated, even if consciously so and by force of will power—and this is of far more worth than any conceivable external aid. Like all writers he is complex, but he keeps his warring selves in line. He is the boss and his body—muscles, endocrines, etc.—, his memories, his aspirations, had better not forget to punch the time clock or to refrain from making too many outside calls.

There is something wrong when a writer is hurried. He is not writing in the present—and he should be. Hurry is synonymous with tension and writing-tension is compounded of anxieties concerning past writing difficulties or past problems or upsets and fears about one's writing future. It is only possible for the relaxed person to write in the present—and this kind of writing is confident, pleasurable writing.

And all the rationalizations for not writing stem from pain of one sort or another. They are many and well known. Durable and a face-saver is the one about not having time. Weaker, transparent and too easily remedied is the need for a sharp pencil or an uncovered typewriter. (How can you possibly create if the typewriter's keys are covered?) The rationalization, however, that has stature is the claim that all writing is futile. This is especially apt during time of war. "How can I write a frothy well-paying boy-meets-girl," it is asked, "while the bombs burst in air and people are being killed."

Now, as of this moment, though the world is not at war, the threat of complete annihilation offers a wonderful excuse not to write—or brush one's teeth or continue a diet or ask for a raise or etc. The excuse—give the devil his due—certainly appears legitimate. But you must remember, if you're going to write—especially prolifically—you must determine that you will have nothing to do with all excuses for not writing—even those of high caliber.

One writer told me that when he starts making excuses, he tells himself, "But you haven't got a toothache," and he finds this reminder irrefutable.

To make all this sort of thing unnecessary, you should recognize and cultivate the pleasures of writing. They do exist—unquestionably. And they are usually not the ordinary pleasures. You must face the fact that writers are more often neurotic than normal. Therefore you must, paradoxically, face your turbulences with equanimity. You must—again paradoxically—be content to be upset. Understanding people, and especially having compassion for them, partakes of serenity, but also of pain. And in spite of all the anguish you may feel (see Thomas Wolfe's "The Story of a Novel"), your lot will seem the only desirable one. And though you may at times wish you were not you, you really do not believe this. You are, in short, somewhat happy in your unhappiness.

And when you're in the midst of writing a book, it's like being in love. All you can think about is your beloved, your book. You have, as in love, your high and your low points, acceptance, rejection. You shuttle, as in love, between ecstasy and despair.

And your pleasure is the ineffable pleasure of creativity. Writing to some degree is an end in itself. It is not merely a means to publication day, reviews, dispensing autographs, and acquiring money. The pleasure in the work itself should at least equal the anticipation of monetary reward and glory. For if there is only this anticipation, ultimately there may only be disappointment.

So the writer if he is to function as a writer

must be a big person. He must have ego, and yet be humble. Always youthfully alert and eager to know more and more so that he be able to understand just a little bit more, and with this increased understanding he will feel greater compassion.

If this is your nature—be it innate or acquired —you won't be afraid of solitude, because no matter how complete it might be, you with all your resources will be there. (So the outcry that writing means painful solitude may be a specious one.)

Success, should it happen, won't turn your head and your point of view or even go so far as to destroy you.

And you will know humility. The quantity of your output, if it is considerable, will mean that you are functioning as a writer and you will not let your ego interpret this in any other way. That you are extremely mortal will be with you night and day. And gnawing at you will also be the knowledge that best-sellers are mortal, too. A few hundred years, after all, is not even a moment in time.

And you will feel that what literary gifts you have—and the power to do something with them, for that matter—have been mysteriously given to you. Feeling this, you will also feel the urges of noblesse oblige. Twain made people laugh, Dickens stirred his time to do something about injustices, and Mencken wrote this epitaph for himself, "If, after I depart this vale, you ever remember me and have thought to please my ghost, forgive some sinner and wink your eye at some homely girl."

Even if you are not moved by such high motivations, even if your raison d'etre is of baser stuff, you should always write the best you can. You shouldn't feel that what is currently being published is bad and that your writing is every bit as bad and should therefore be published. Editors sometimes have to use what they prefer to call "adequate" stories. I know that I have been guilty of this—of necessity. Don't emulate these adequate or inferior stories.

Never write down; it can't be done—successfully. It can't be done prolifically or pleasantly. How awful to sit down before your typewriter and say, "Well, now I'm going to write a bad story." In such a situation, you dare not be enthusiastic, because then the story may turn out to be good; or get inside the characters and feel as they feel; or enjoy what you write; or rewrite and rewrite and polish and polish.

To repeat, write the best that you can at all times. A genre may have certain limitations—and editors may insist you stay within them—but write the best that you can within the genre. You should even strive for originality, which is not esoteric, but merely doing something your way, when your way differs from the way it's being done. Originality, in a particular instance, may be better or worse than accepted practice. But it is being yourself. And that, when you get right down to it, is most important.